Contents

MW01041620

Part 1

The Arab World before 1914

1 Travelling in the Ottoman Empire

Up to 1918 the Ottoman Empire (with its capital at Constantinople in Turkey) had two huge provinces in the Middle East. Syria was administered from Damascus and covered the area to the west. In the east was Mesopotamia with its headquarters in Baghdad. Most of its people lived on marshes or irrigated land beside the rivers Tigris and Euphrates. Between these provinces lay the desert region of Arabia which stretched far to the south. Most of its people were nomadic Arabs or Beduin.

Travellers in the Ottoman Empire often used the old routes followed by traders leading their camels loaded with spices. The author of Source B took a caravan route to Roman ruins at Palmyra in 1889. In 1895 a railway was built to link Beirut with Damascus and Gertrude Bell travelled on it in 1911 (Source C). The authors of Source D describe how they used the keleg, a raft made of thin poles, boards and inflated sheepskins for their voyage down the river Tigris from Mosul to Baghdad.

A Syria and Mesopotamia before 1914

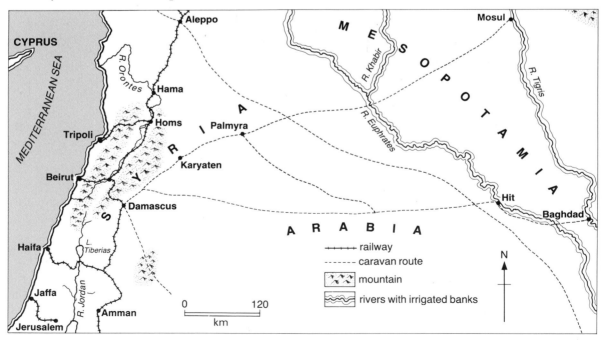

B Into the desert

From G. Hill, *With the Beduins*, T. Fisher Unwin, 1891.

At Karyaten the waterless desert begins and extends to Palmyra ... The Governor of Karyaten said we must take four soldiers with us, as the desert was not safe from the predatory* Beduins ... We had engaged three camels to carry water for ourselves, our men and our animals, and a man with a long firelock gun accompanied them as driver. ...

* thieving

We left the gardens and the cypress trees behind us, and then through the haze of the Sirocco* we went out as it were into space, and lost sight of everything but our own men and the ground beneath our feet ... The moon was at the full, but the dull hot wind blew across our faces, and we breathed with difficulty.

* a dry desert wind

C Beirut to Damascus Railway

From G. L. Bell, *Blackwood's Magazine*, Blackwood and Sons, April 1911.

Immediately after leaving Rayyak ... tiny villages huddled against the flanks of hills had a familiar air; in spite of the railway they are still very remote from civilization and their inhabitants belong to a Moslem sect which is noted for fanaticism and ignorance. But the prospect changed when we topped the summit of the pass and ran down to Zebedani, famous for its apples ... past Douma, where wealthy Damascenes have built among gardens their summer resorts ... and out into the plain of Damascus.

D Down the Tigris

From W. A. and E. T. A. Wigram, *The Cradle of Mankind*, A. and C. Black, 1914.

A raft voyage is probably the most absolutely restful mode of travel known, if only the wanderer is in no hurry to reach his destination; ... from Mosul to Baghdad the quickest voyage ever known was two days and a half, and the longest fourteen ... You lie on your camp bed under the shade of your grass hut, watching the shore slide past your sleepy eyes ... Slowly the last stage of the journey is accomplished ... Date groves appear on the shore in place of melon gardens ... Finally 'Baghdad's walls of fretted gold' are seen in the distance.

Questions

1 What present-day states occupy the area of the map?

2 Explain the two dangers for travellers referred to in B.

3 What do you learn from Source C about different styles of living in Syria?

4 Why might it take two, or fourteen, days to travel by raft from Mosul to Baghdad?

5 What do the sources and map tell you about the problems faced by the Turkish government in controlling their empire?

3

2 Beduin of the desert

The Beduin are Arab nomads. In the nineteenth century, Beduin roamed most of the badia, *or drier regions, of the Middle East with their herds of camels or flocks of sheep and goats. Shortage of grazing land and water had caused them to split into tribes. Each tribe had its own* dira, *or grazing district, agreed with neighbouring Beduin. The Adwan, visited by Gray Hill, an English traveller, in the spring of 1888, was a smaller Beduin tribe who lived in the grassland to the east of the meeting point of the River Jordan and the Dead Sea. Like other tribes, the Adwan was ruled by a leader elected by the* shaykhs, *or men of authority, who acted as his council.*

Beduin tribes had war-like reputations and defended their territory fiercely, often refusing to pay taxes. In the 1860s the Turkish government tried to force the Beduin in Syria to accept their rule. At first they met with little success, and caravans and travellers passing across Beduin territory were raided by tribes unless safe passage was paid for. Hill agreed a contract for an armed escort with an agent of the Adwan before setting out from Jerusalem to visit them. The Beduin feast described in the passage was not only an important social occasion, but also an example of the hospitality a Beduin shaykh might provide for friendly visitors.

A   An important occasion

The tent was about eighty feet long, open on the whole length of that side of it which looked towards the valley, except for one end which contained the apartment of the women. . . .

Ali Diab sat on a carpet with his back towards the closed back of the tent, his youngest son on his right, and his nephew on his left, and the more important members of the tribe near to him. Others were placed according to their several ranks in the estimation of the tribe on carpets laid opposite to, and on each side of him, so as to form a small square. In the middle of this square was a heap of hot wood ashes, from which an old slave picked live embers, which he held with a pair of little tongs to any one who wished to light narghile* or cigarette. Ali Diab sent for some cushions from the women's apartment to be put at our backs, beautiful Persian rugs having already been spread where we sat. Our place was on the shaykh's left, next to the nephew. The tent was full of people, and just in front of it the shaykh's mare was tethered; many Beduins came and went, sitting, smoking, staring at us for a little while, and then departing as if to make room for more; and when an important man came into the little square Ali Diab rose up in honour of the comer, and all rose with him.

Lemonade was brought in a bowl, and then poured into glasses, and little cups of coffee without sugar (Beduin fashion) were handed about, first to us, and then to the rest sitting in the square . . . Ali Diab was silent, and we enjoyed sitting still and looking about us. Presently a

From G. Hill, *With the Beduins*, T. Fisher Unwin, 1891.

*a tobacco-pipe

great bowl was brought in containing a whole sheep stuffed with rice and pistachio nuts, excellently cooked, and laid upon Arab loaves of bread made in the form of pancakes. A few spoons were stuck into it for our use, and we were invited to be the first to put our hands in the dish. With some anxiety we did so, but found it very good – a most savoury mess. We forebore to eat more than two mouthfuls, however, wishing to acquire a reputation for good breeding, and when we had eaten, Ali Diab motioned to the Beduins to draw near. . . . The most important ate first, and were followed by the others according to their degrees, and in a very short time the great mass of food had disappeared.

One of the head men told us that he would like to go to England. We asked him what he would do there. He explained that he should first go to stay with the Queen, and then he would go to visit Napoleon, King of France. The Beduins do not read the newspapers, and he was a little behind the time. No doubt he thought that the Queen and Napoleon III lived in great tents like Ali Diab, where all could come and go at pleasure, and eat of the hospitable dish.

George whispered to us that the shaykh had killed two sheep in our honour, and that we must, according to Beduin custom, make him a suitable present; so, having nothing with us, we asked the shaykh's son to come back with us to visit us in our tent. He came, and we gave him a small revolver, which he took away rejoicing.

Questions

1 Can you think why the gift of a revolver would delight the shaykh's son?

2 Is there any evidence in the source which tells you about the position of women in Beduin society?

3 List in descending order of importance those present at the feast. What evidence in the passage has influenced your placing of each person or group?

4 Why did the Beduin head man think that if he went to England he would stay with the Queen?

5 Suggest some reasons for the head man being 'a little behind the time'.

6 What would be the main differences between a Beduin feast and a royal banquet at Buckingham Palace? Might there be any similarities?

3 Villagers of the Nile

Egypt was the most populated country in the Middle East in 1882 when it was occupied by Britain and separated from the Ottoman Empire. Four fifths of her approximately 7 million people were peasants living in the valley and delta of the River Nile. They cultivated cotton and sugar-cane as well as cereal crops. For all these they depended on the Nile for water and on its annual flooding, or inundation, which gave their fields a fresh covering of soil each year. Their methods are described in Source B by Stanley Lane-Poole, an archaeologist and professor of Arabic who visited Egypt frequently in the later nineteenth century. Source A is one of the illustrations in his book which were usually based on artists' sketches of places visited by him before the days when it was possible to print photographs in books and newspapers.

There was very little factory production in Egypt at that time. Skilled craftsmen of the type observed by Klunzinger, a German doctor who worked as a health officer in southern Egypt in the 1860s and 1870s (Source C), formed the backbone of industry in the villages and towns.

A   *Shaduf*

An artist's engraving of one of two main ways of raising water from the Nile. Water-wheels were the other

B The *fellah*

The agricultural population . . . is known as the 'fellahin', whereof the singular is fellah, and means literally a 'cleaver' or 'cutter' of the ground, and hence a peasant . . . 'Waterer' would be a better name than 'cleaver' for the Egyptian peasant since, under the present antiquated system, he is watering the ground from morning till night . . . But for this difficulty of irrigation and keeping up canals the Egyptian peasant would have an easy time of it . . . The one thing that can make or mar his crops is the annual inundations: a 'good Nile' . . . 'a bad Nile' . . . Beyond this one vital element in Egyptian agriculture there is no natural cause to dread . . . The whole process is as simple as possible, the cultivator has only to see that the alluvial deposit has been spread over the land, to pass a light primitive plough over it, scatter the wheat or barley seed, keep the birds off the young crops, cut them when ripe with the old fashioned sickle, thresh them with a curious crushing cart with heavy iron wheels, winnow them by throwing them up in the air, and the grain is ready for the mill.

From S. Lane-Poole, *Social Life in Egypt*, J. S. Virtue and Co., 1884.

C The craftsman

The cabinet-maker or carpenter . . . has neither a bench, nor in general a vice . . . He squats upon the board he is to plane and hew . . . Instead of a rule he is generally satisfied with a cord or a palm twig, on which he marks his measurements . . . His boring tool resembles the instrument of the pipe-maker . . .

It can at once be told, however, whether an article has been made by an Arab or a European. The natives know this very well themselves, and have a keen sense of their own inferiority in such matters. An Arab chair never quite stands firm on its feet, a table or a door is always a little off the truth . . .

From C. B. Klunzinger, *Upper Egypt: Its Peoples and Its Products*, Blackie and Sons, 1878.

Questions

1 Explain the meaning of 'a good Nile' and 'a bad Nile'.

2 What does the picture tell you about the work of Egyptian peasant women?

3 How did the chain of shadufs work?

4 Why do you think the shaduf survived for so long?

5 Suggest reasons for the comment in Source C that begins 'The natives know this very well . . .'

6 In which ways were the methods and equipment used by the peasant and the carpenter 'antiquated'?

7 Describe how a more modern craftsman might improve on the work of the carpenter.

4 Homes in Egypt and Lebanon

Egypt's towns and villages were built near to the banks of the river Nile. A town consisted of a maze of streets, with mostly single-storied houses each with its own courtyard. Leading off the courtyard of a wealthier Egyptian's home might be a room described in Source A by C.B. Klunzinger who lived in southern Egypt in the 1860s and 1870s.

Most families lived in small villages. In Source B Klunzinger describes the house of a poorer peasant, or fellah. The photograph was taken later by an American missionary living in Beirut. It shows a different kind of peasant's house in the Mount Lebanon district in the west of Turkish Syria.

A Town house

We enter a well lighted and spacious saloon. . . . The floor consists of . . . a mass of clay and sand smoothed . . . and hardened almost to the consistency of marble. The walls are white-washed, . . . have numerous niches, and are adorned with a few verses of the Koran* framed and glazed, here and there also with sheets of pictures of Arabic or Frankish* production. . . . The ceiling is composed of . . . the midribs of palm fronds, with a coating of clay and lime above. In the houses of wealthier persons we find an artistic panelled ceiling of mosaic. We are glad to observe there is no glass in the windows . . . and much prefer the cool air streaming in through unglazed apertures. . . .

Across the far end of the room runs a low band of stone or clay projecting several feet. Over the mattress . . . is spread a bright coloured cloth or carpet hanging down in folds in front. The cushions . . . lie at fixed intervals . . . and thus the famous DIVAN is formed. On the floor along the sides of the room a splendid Persian carpet is spread over a straw mat . . . No other furniture or utensils are here except some water-coolers on window ledges, shelves or niches in the wall, and religious manuscripts with black, red and gold letters.

From C. B. Klunzinger, *Upper Egypt: Its Peoples and Its Products*, Blackie and Sons, 1878.

* the Muslim holy book

* from western Europe

B *Fellah's* house

. . . the fellah kneads for himself a hovel out of the clay left by the Nile in every hollow, mixed with some cut straw. A room is thus formed which may be entered by creeping through a hole. It is covered over with reeds, straw mats and rags. Round it he then builds a wall of clay about as high as a man, which incloses a yard. Cylindrical hollow spaces . . . are let into the wall at intervals, and serve for keeping grain, . . . as a pigeon-house, fowl-house, an oven, and a cupboard . . . Poverty, of course, breeds dirt: in an earthen burrow which has to shelter a numerous family . . . and which serves as a sitting room and bed-room, as kitchen, dining room, and stable, it is not expected that

From C. B. Klunzinger, *Upper Egypt: Its Peoples and Its Products*, Blackie and Sons, 1878.

wall and floor should shine . . . The curious visitor will probably find the external walls thickly plastered with cow-dung, which serves as fuel for baking and cooking. . . .

C A house in a Lebanese village

The peasant woman seated in the centre is feeding a sheep with mulberry leaves

Questions

1 How does Source A suggest that the owner of the house is both educated and well-off?

2 Why do the Egyptian houses have few pieces of furniture?

3 How did home-builders take Egypt's climate into account?

4 Why is the Lebanese house and its surroundings built on two levels?

5 What similarities are there in the materials and construction of roofs of the houses in Sources B and C?

6 Does the picture provide any evidence that the Lebanese peasant's house is more advanced than the Egyptian peasant's?

7 Explain the differences in materials and construction of walls in all the houses.

8 Can you find anything in Klunzinger's descriptions that suggest he was more likely to have visited the inside of a town house than a peasant's house?

5 Muslim worship

Most Arabs are Muslims who are members of Islam and followers of its founder, the prophet Mohammed. 'Islam' means belief in complete surrender to Allah, or God. Muslims pray five times a day and worship at a mosque once a week if they can. The photograph is of the Sultan Hassan Madrassa Mosque in Cairo. The recess, or mihrab, in the wall shows worshippers the direction of Mecca. Each Friday a sermon is preached from the minbar, or pulpit, next to the mihrab.

Mecca, the birthplace of Mohammed, was a meeting place for traders until Mohammed captured it in AD 630 and turned it into the religious centre of Islam. The most important religious experience for a Muslim is a pilgrimage, or haj, to Mecca. Arabs will be joined by pilgrims from the other Islamic peoples such as those from Afghanistan and modern Pakistan and Bangladesh. In about 1930 the Afghan writer of Source B went on his pilgrimage, spending ten days praying at the holy places. He describes his preparations during the journey and his visit to the courtyard of al-Haram mosque in which stands the Ka'bah, the Muslims' holiest shrine. The Ka'bah is probably the remains of a meteorite which, Muslims say, was given to Adam to gain forgiveness for his sins after his fall from paradise. The Ka'bah is built into one wall of a cube-shaped building covered for most of the year with a black curtain embroidered with verses from the Koran.

A Mihrab and minbar

B Pilgrimage to Mecca

The city is open only to Muslims, and my recent visit to the mystic shrines of that veiled town of the desert has left very vivid impressions upon my mind . . . From Jeddah, our long caravan journeyed Mecca-ward. With my head shaven and wearing only one white sheet, the pilgrim's costume, I nestled down in my mat-covered litter which was tied on the back of my camel. The rocking movement to and fro of my litter kept time with the recitation of ninety-nine names of Allah. 'I am in Thy Presence, O, the Mighty', I prayed and my tongue seemed to cling to the roof of my mouth with thirst, but imbued with an intense feeling of religious fervour, I continued, 'Lead me in Thine own way, O Allah, as I approach Thy Throne' . . .

I waited in the sullen heat while the sun beat down on my shaven head, till I found room to approach the holy precincts. Thousands of pilgrims packed the Haram Sharief, or the Great Mosque, waiting to kiss the mystic Black Stone which, set in silver, is built in a wall of a small room covered by the Carpet. Around this structure wide marble floor is laid, on which the faithful walk as they encircle the Ka'bah seven times on entering the Mosque. In the midst of this vast quadrangle of some 280 paces long and 80 paces broad, surrounded as it is by the double arches of the colonnades, stood the Ka'bah, where the bending and swaying of the worshippers . . . as they faced the heart of the Mosque, or clung to curtains of the mystic Ka'bah, appeared to me a world of its own.

From Sirdar Ikbal Ali Shah, *The Golden East*, John Long Ltd., 1931.

Questions

1 Identify the mihrab and minbar in the photograph.

2 Why is the mihrab always empty?

3 The stairs and seat in the minbar are forbidden to all. Why do you think this is?

4 In what ways does the writer in Source B prepare himself for his entry to Mecca?

5 Why do you think he refers to Mecca as 'that veiled town of the desert'?

6 From Source B, what clues can you find about the importance of a pilgrimage to Mecca to a devout Muslim?

7 What evidence is there in the sources that prayer is important to a Muslim?

8 How would you describe the differences between and similarities in furnishings and architecture of a mosque and a Christian church?

6 A Mosque school

For centuries most education in Egypt had gone no further than teaching the Koran, or holy book, to boys only. This had hardly changed by the late nineteenth century, even though some rulers of Egypt wanted to introduce science and technology into schools.

Source A is a description of the school attached to the Mosque of Sultan Hasan in Cairo. It is written by Lane-Poole, the archaeologist who wrote Source B in Unit 3. The illustration is a steel engraving from Lane-Poole's book, similar to the source in Unit 3.

A The schoolroom

When the boy is five or six years old he is sent to the public school. An institution of this kind is attached to almost every mosque and drinking fountain in Cairo and the country towns . . . It consists of a single room, where the pupils . . . squat in rows before the schoolmaster, and are duly provided, for a very trifling payment, with what passes for a polite education in Egypt. This consists, first, in learning the alphabet, which the master writes out in bold characters on a small white board, which the pupil holds in his hands. Next, reading is taught by easy stages, but very often this accomplishment is never properly acquired, and the pupil passes on to learning the Koran, or part of the Koran, by heart. To be able to recite certain portions of the Koran is essential to the due performance of the rites of religion; whereas most people can get on in Egypt very well without being proficient in reading. Hence the learning of the Koran is the chief business of the school, and reading is directed mainly to that end. The pupil is given a chapter of the sacred book, opened out on a little desk made of palm sticks, and proceeds to commit it to memory by chanting it aloud in a sing-song fashion, swinging the body to and fro to the rhythm of the verses. It is not difficult to ascertain when a school is at work: the babel of confused noise which proceeds from the simultaneous chanting of different portions of the Koran by the various scholars is audible at some distance.

This is all that the boy generally learns at school. Indeed, the schoolmaster could not teach him much more. The worthy man knows his Koran, and can instil it, with the help of a stout cane into his pupils' skulls; but he is thoroughly illiterate, and sometimes cannot even read, and has to get a pupil-teacher to write the alphabets and copies, on the pretence of having himself weak eyes. Writing is not usually taught at a school, and the lower classes do not feel any urgent necessity for this accomplishment. Public writers are always to be had if a letter has to be indited* on rate occasions. Arithmetic and anything beyond 'the three R's' must be acquired from other masters.

From S. Lane-Poole, *Social Life in Egypt*, J. S. Virtue and Co., 1884.

* *written*

12

B A room in the school of Sultan Hasan

Questions

1 In the picture what task is being performed by the boy sitting alone in front of the schoolmaster?

2 What does the writer mean when he describes the lessons as 'what passes for a polite education'?

3 What evidence is there in Sources A and B that discipline was strict?

4 Can you think of reasons why a Koranic school at a drinking fountain might be different from one attached to a mosque?

5 Girls rarely attended Koranic schools. Why do you think this was?

6 What are the advantages and disadvantages as historical evidence of specially drawn engravings, compared with photographs?

7 Can you suggest reasons why the Egyptian government in fact found it difficult to bring education closer to that of western Europe?

8 In which ways do you think schools such as these matched other features of Egyptian society in the nineteenth century?

Part 2

Collapse of the Ottoman Empire

7 Turkey goes to war

The map (Source B) was drawn for a British newspaper in 1913. It shows how Turks felt that their empire was under pressure from Russia and Britain. Russia hoped to gain control of Constantinople so her ships could sail into the Mediterranean without risk from Turkish guns at the entrance to the Black Sea. Britain had a protectorate over the oil-rich country of Koweit (or Kuwait) and British oil and railway companies were busy in Persia (or Iran). Readers of the newspaper would not need to be told that Britain also ruled Egypt where she owned the Suez canal.

In reply to these threats the Turks granted Germany the right to build a railway through their Arab empire. It was spoken of as 'the Berlin-Baghdad railway' but the map shows it was planned to go on to Basra. Very little of the railway was built by 1914 but Germany and Turkey were close enough to sign a secret alliance in August. In November, German warships, flying the Turkish flag, shelled Russian ports on the Black Sea. Russia, Britain and France, the Entente countries, then declared war on Turkey.

In Source A, Djemal Pasha, Turkey's naval minister, explains why he supported his country's entry into the war. He speaks of her relations with Britain and Russia and also with France who had many business interests in Syria and hoped to win control of it.

A   A Turkish minister remembers

There is one fact that no one in the world can deny – that Russia is the hereditary enemy of the Ottoman Empire, and that her greatest desire is the possession of Constantinople . . . Her allies, so far from opposing her design, were . . . entirely in agreement . . . England, mistress of Egypt, looked with far more jealous eyes at Germany's economic plans in the Gulf of Basra than at Russia's ambitions . . . As for France, she was not one of those who would oppose the partition of Turkey so long as she was given a free hand in Syria.

. . . Germany, whatever else might be said, was the ONLY power which desired to see Turkey strong . . . Germany regarded Turkey as a link in the commercial and trading chain, and thus became her stoutest champion against the Entente* governments which wanted to dismember her, particularly as the elimination of Turkey would mean the final 'encirclement' of Germany.

From Djemal Pasha, Memories of a Turkish Statesman, George H. Doran Company, 1922.

* Britain, France and Russia

14

... in my view, rather than fall miserably under the yoke of the Russians, English and French, after the Russians had won, it was infinitely better to defend ourselves to the last drop of blood in the hope of freeing ourselves for ever – the only alternative worthy of a brave and great nation ...

B

Turkey and her neighbours

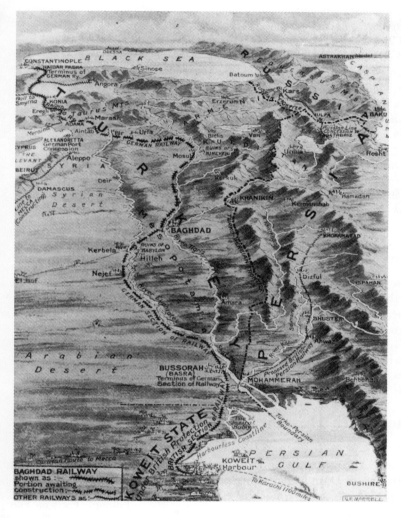

Questions

1 From Source A, list a) the threats seen by Djemal Pasha, and b) the reasons he gives for German friendliness to Turkey.

2 How does the map a) support Djemal's fears, b) show the value of the railway, and c) explain the importance of Constantinople?

8 Wartime agreements

Turkey's entry into the First World War gave the Arab peoples a chance to break away from her empire. The Arab who took the lead was Husain ibn Ali, ruler of the Hejaz in western Arabia. As a member of the Hashemite royal family which was descended from the prophet Mohammed he was also Sharif of Mecca so most Muslims recognised him as head of their faith.

In November 1914, Husain, supported by his sons, Faisal and Abdullah, refused to back Turkey in her war. The British quickly wrote to Abdullah promising support for the Arabs if they helped the Entente.

In the second half of 1915, Husain negotiated secretly with Britain through her ambassador in Cairo, Sir Henry MacMahon. Source A is part of the proposal for Arab independence that Husain asked MacMahon to sign. Source B shows that MacMahon agreed with Husain's proposals with a few exceptions. While MacMahon was talking to Husain, other secret negotiations were taking place between British and French officials, Mark Sykes and Georges Picot, to draw up spheres of interest for their two countries to take up when Turkey was defeated. Sykes and Picot also added an international area. The map is based on the one drawn by the officials in 1916. The details of the Sykes–Picot Agreement were kept secret until Russia's Bolshevik revolutionary government made them public in November 1917.

A Sharif Husain to Sir Henry MacMahon, 14 July, 1915.

1 Great Britain recognises the independence of the Arab countries which are bounded: on the north, by the line Mersin–Adana to parallel 37°N and thence along the line Birejik–Urfa–Mardin–Midiat–Jazirat–Amadia to the Persian frontier; on the east, by the Persian frontier down to the Persian Gulf; on the south, by the Indian Ocean (with the exclusion of Aden whose status will remain as at present); on the west, by the Red Sea and the Mediterranean Sea back to Mersin.

From G. Antonius, *The Arab Awakening*, Hamish Hamilton, 1938.

B Sir Henry MacMahon to Sharif Husain, 24 October, 1915.

The two districts of Mersina and Alexandretta and portions of Syria lying to the west of the districts of Damascus, Homs, Hama and Aleppo cannot be said to be purely Arab, and should be excluded from the limits demanded. . .

As for those regions lying within those frontiers wherein Great Britain is free to act without detriment to the interests of her ally, France, I am empowered in the name of the Government of Great Britain to give the following assurances and make the following reply to your letter:

1) Subject to the above modifications, Great Britain is prepared to recognise and support the independence of the Arabs in all the regions within the limits demanded by the Sharif of Mecca.

From W. Laqueur and B. Rubin (eds.), *The Israel-Arab Reader* (4th Edition), Facts on File Publications, 1985.

2) Great Britain will guarantee the Holy Places against all external aggression and will recognise their inviolability.

C   The Sykes–Picot Agreement, May 1916

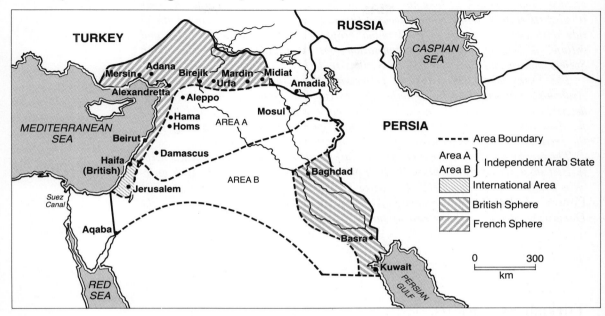

Questions

1 Make your own outline map marking the coasts and rivers. Draw in the boundaries for Arab countries proposed by Husain in Source A. Shade in the area you think MacMahon refers to in the first paragraph of Source B.

2 What hint does MacMahon give that Palestine might also not be recognised as an area of Arab independence?

3 Describe the most important differences between the Husain–MacMahon Agreement (Source B) and the Sykes–Picot Agreement (Source C).

4 Why did Britain wish to control the area shown as her sphere of interest? (See Sources A and B, Unit 7.)

5 An Arab historian described the Sykes–Picot Agreement as the outcome of 'greed' and 'stupidity'. What arguments might support the claim that it was a) greedy and b) stupid?

6 Imagine an argument between an Arab leader and a British foreign office official after the Sykes–Picot Agreement was published. How would one attack the Agreement and the other defend it?

9 The Arab revolt, 1916–18

Even though Husain refused to back Turkey, an Arab revolt did not break out at the beginning of the First World War. One reason was that the Arabs were divided. Some wished to take the chance to persuade Turkey to reform the way it ruled its empire, while others favoured the nationalist goal of replacing Turkish rule with independent states built round people sharing the same language and culture. A leading nationalist organisation was Al Fatat, or the Young Arab Society, which had been founded by Syrians in 1911.

The Turks made the mistake of persecuting the nationalists. In Source A an Arab historian tells how two groups were executed in Damascus and Beirut and describes the reaction of Prince Faisal, Husain's youngest son, who had pleaded for their lives with Djemal Pasha, a Turkish government minister. Shortly after the executions, Husain declared the Arabs' revolt against Turkish rule.

The Arabs could do little against the Turks without British and French help. A British secret agent, Captain T. E. Lawrence, went on raids with Arab guerrilla bands in 1917 and 1918. In Source B, which is from his memoirs, Seven Pillars of Wisdom, *Lawrence tells of an attack on a section of the Damascus–Medina railway east of the Red Sea port of Aqaba.*

A Turkish executions, 1916

The sentences had not been announced beforehand. On the eve of the execution, a gaoler had entered the hall of the prison at 'Aley and read out the names of twenty-one of the accused, bidding them dress and follow him. Those for Damascus were taken by train and, on arrival there, marched to the Marjeh – the main square – where seven gallows stood in readiness. The others were driven down to Beirut in carriages, and guessing their fate, whiled hours of darkness away with hymns to Arab freedom, one cab-load answering another, until, as dawn was breaking, the convoy came to a halt in Liberty Square. By six o'clock that morning – the 6th of May 1916 – the holocaust was over, and within two hours a special number of *al-Sharq** was being distributed free, in which the charges, the trials, the sentences and the executions were announced in the same breath. The charges were defined as 'treasonable participation in activities of which the aims were to separate Syria, Palestine and Iraq from the Ottoman Sultanate, and to constitute them into an independent State.'

. . . Faisal was deeply affected. He had gone beyond the bounds of prudence in pleading with Djemal for the lives of the Arab patriots. Whatever doubts may have lingered in his mind as to the wisdom of breaking with the Turks were now swept away in a passionate revulsion of feeling, and the cry which escaped him on hearing the news of the executions became the battle-cry of the Arab revolt.

From G. Antonius, *The Arab Awakening*, Hamish Hamilton, 1938.

** a government newspaper*

B Train blown up, 6 October 1917

When Faiz and Bedri* heard the engine over their arch, they danced   *Arab guerrillas
a war-dance round their little electric box. The Arabs in the ditch were
hissing softly to me that it was time to fire: but not until the engine
was exactly over the arch did I jump up and wave my cloak. Faiz
instantly pressed his handle, and the great noise and dust and black-
ness burst up . . . Our mine had taken out the rear arch of the bridge.
Of the locomotive, the fire-box was torn open, and many tubes burst
. . . The tender and first wagon had telescoped. About twenty Turks
were dead, and others prisoners, including four officers, who stood by
the line weeping for the life which the Arabs had no mind to take.

The contents of the trucks were food stuffs, some seventy tons of
them; 'urgently needed', according to the way-bill, in Medain Salih.
We sent one way-bill to Faisal, as detailed report of our success . . .

My pupils practised the art of mining afterwards by themselves, and
taught others . . . In the next four months our experts from Akaba
destroyed seventeen locomotives. Travelling became an uncertain
terror for the enemy. At Damascus people scrambled for the back seat
in trains, even paid extra for them. The engine-drivers struck. Civilian
traffic nearly ceased; and we extended our threat to Aleppo by the
mere posting a notice one night in Damascus Town Hall, that good
Arabs would henceforward travel by the Syrian railway at their own
risk. The loss of the engines was sore upon the Turks. Since the rolling
stock was pooled for Palestine and Hejaz, our destructions not merely   From T. E. Lawrence,
made the mass evacuation of Medina impossible, but began to pinch   *Seven Pillars of Wisdom,*
the army about Jerusalem, just as the British threat grew formidable.   Jonathan Cape, 1935.

Questions

1 What evidence is there in
Source A that the Turks
ruled their empire in a
repressive way in 1916?

2 Can you think of reasons
why Faisal might have 'gone
beyond the bounds of
prudence' in trying to save
the accused?

3 Does Source B provide a clue
to Faisal's importance to
military operations during the
revolt?

4 What was the 'little electric
box' in Source B?

5 Pick out from Source B
examples of subversive
activity carried out by Arabs
against the Turks.

6 From Source B, what do you
think was T. E. Lawrence's
role as a British agent?

7 What was the value of the
operation described by
Lawrence to the British
campaign against Turkey?

10 A Jewish home in Palestine?

In 1914 there were about 600,000 Arabs in Palestine and about 80,000 Jews. Few of these Palestinian Jews were Zionists who believed in a national home for the Jewish people. On the other hand, Jewish leaders in Europe were becoming increasingly Zionist. Since 1905 the World Zionist Congress had been campaigning for the national home to be in Palestine. In the First World War the Zionists saw a chance to get support. Their campaigns centred on Britain. Her politicians were also looking for ways of encouraging breakaway movements in the German and Austrian empires where the greatest number of European Jews lived. Britain's allies, especially the USA, supported this policy.

The President of the English Zionist Federation, Dr. Chaim Weizmann, knew A. J. Balfour, the Foreign Secretary. In June 1917 Balfour asked the Federation to draft a proposal on the future of Palestine which he could put to the Cabinet. Source A is from the draft proposal. In Source B, a Jewish member of the Cabinet, Edwin Montagu, who was not a Zionist, puts a different view. Source C is from the Cabinet minutes and shows how Balfour put the case for supporting Zionism. Chaim Weizmann was waiting outside and the news that the cabinet had agreed was brought out to him, he says, by Mark Sykes, the Cabinet's assistant secretary (Source D). On 2 November, Balfour wrote to Lord Rothschild, a leading member of the Zionist Federation, to tell him of the Cabinet decision (Source E).

A The Zionist proposal

1 His Majesty's Government accepts the principle that Palestine should be reconstituted as the National Home of the Jewish people.
2 His Majesty's Government will use its best endeavours to secure the achievement of this object and will discuss the necessary methods and means with the Zionist Organization.

From R. Sanders, *The High Walls of Jerusalem*, Holt, Rinehart and Winston, 1983.

B A non-Zionist's doubts

If a Jewish Englishman . . . longs for the day when he can shake British soil from his shoes and go back to agricultural pursuits in Palestine he has always seemed to me to have acknowledged aims inconsistent with British citizenship . . . .

From R. Sanders, *The High Walls of Jerusalem*, Holt, Rinehart and Winston, 1983.

C Balfour puts the case in Cabinet, 31 October 1917

. . . from a purely diplomatic and political point of view it was desirable that some declaration favourable to the aspiration of the Jewish nationalists should now be made . . . If we could make a declaration favourable to such an ideal, we should be able to carry on an extremely useful propaganda both in Russia and America.

From T. G. Fraser (ed.), *The Middle East, 1914–1979*, Edward Arnold, 1980.

D Weizmann hears the news

While the Cabinet was in session, approving the final text, I was waiting outside . . . Sykes brought the document out to me, with the exclamation:

'Dr. Weizmann, it's a boy!' Well – I did not like the boy at first. He was not the one I expected. But I knew this was a great event.

From C. Weizmann, *Trial and Error*, Hamish Hamilton, 1949.

E The Balfour Declaration

Foreign Office,
November 2nd, 1917.

Dear Lord Rothschild,

I have much pleasure in conveying to you, on behalf of His Majesty's Government, the following declaration of sympathy with Jewish Zionist aspirations which has been submitted to, and approved by, the Cabinet.

"His Majesty's Government view with favour the establishment in Palestine of a national home for the Jewish people, and will use their best endeavours to facilitate the achievement of this object, it being clearly understood that nothing shall be done which may prejudice the civil and religious rights of existing non-Jewish communities in Palestine, or the rights and political status enjoyed by Jews in any other country".

I should be grateful if you would bring this declaration to the knowledge of the Zionist Federation.

Questions

1 How might you know that Source A was meant to be discussed by the Cabinet?

2 From Source A, what three things were the Zionists hoping the government would do?

3 Put arguments for and against Montagu's view that Zionists could not be good citizens.

4 What had Balfour in mind when he spoke in Source C of the political gains from a Declaration?

5 What did Sykes in D mean by saying 'it's a boy'? From Source E suggest why Weizmann didn't like the boy at first.

6 Compare A and E. List the points in A which the Cabinet a) accepted, and b) changed or added to.

11 The Mandates

In 1916 Sir Mark Sykes and Georges Picot had agreed to divide the Arab parts of the Turkish empire into British and French spheres of influence after the war (see Unit 8). Very shortly after the fighting stopped, the Prime Ministers of the two countries, David Lloyd George and Georges Clemenceau met to discuss the details. One of their meetings is described by the cabinet secretary, Sir Maurice Hankey, in his diary for 4 December 1918 (Source A).

A few months later, the Paris Peace Conference agreed to set up the League of Nations. One of its tasks was to hand over the ex-colonies of defeated Germany and Turkey to the countries which would rule them under mandates. The League laid down that local political leaders should be consulted about which country should be given the mandate. Source B is an extract from the views given to a League commission of enquiry in Syria in July 1919. Syria at that time was often thought of as a large part of the Middle East which included Palestine and Lebanon.

The map shows how the Ottoman empire was divided into mandated territories in May 1920. The Mandates were said to be a means of helping each country to develop a system of government which would make it possible for it to become independent. Many Arabs believed that their real purpose was to give power in the Middle East to France and Britain and there were revolts and disturbances in all the Mandated Territories. In Source D a senior British official tells how he secretly met a group of nationalists in Iraq in June 1920 to explore ways of ending the revolts there.

A Britain and France decide

Ll. G* and Clemenceau had driven to the French embassy . . . When they were alone . . . Clemenceau said: 'Well, what are we to discuss?' 'Mesopotamia and Palestine,' replied Ll. G. 'Tell me what you want,' asked Clemenceau. 'I want Mosul*,' said Ll. G. 'You shall have it,' said Clemenceau. 'Anything else?' 'Yes, I want Jerusalem too', continued Ll. G. 'You shall have it,' said Clemenceau, 'but Pichon will make difficulties about Mosul.' There was absolutely no record or memorandum made at the time, and I believe my diary of Dec 4, 1918 contains the only record . . . and that was only second hand from Ll. G for I was not present.

* Lloyd George

* important for its oilfields

From S. Roskill, *Hankey: Man of Secrets* (vol II), Collins, 1972.

B The Syrian Congress protests

6 We do not acknowledge any right claimed by the French Government in any part whatever of our Syrian country and refuse that she should assist us . . .

7 We oppose the pretensions of the Zionists to create a Jewish commonwealth in the southern part of Syria, known as Palestine . . .

From W. Laqueur and B. Rubin (eds.), *The Israel-Arab Reader* (4th Edition), Facts on File Publications, 1985.

C The League scheme

D Iraqis and British disagree

It was known to the world, they said, that the Mandatory system was a disguised form of annexation . . . We had denied it, but our proceedings in Palestine were not in keeping with our professions*, nor had we hitherto given proof positive of our intention to set up a National Government in Iraq . . . For them, in Iraq to accept anything short of complete independence would be disastrous, for it would involve the acceptance of a similar scheme under French auspices in Syria, and they distrusted the French more than the British.

public statements

I warned them that H.M's Government would be compelled to maintain, or if need be to restore, order by military force – I begged them to realize the bloodshed that this policy must entail. They replied that it would be a small price to pay for independence.

From A. T. Wilson,
Mesopotamia 1917–20,
O.U.P., 1931.

Questions

1 What name was Mesopotamia given as a mandate?

2 Suggest why the two leaders found it easier to agree over Jerusalem than Mosul.

3 Give arguments for and against A being reliable as historical evidence.

4 Explain the two objections of the Syrians to the mandate.

5 List the gains Britain made from her mandates at the time and for the future.

6 Compare Map C with the map on page 17. How had the League of Nations altered the 1916 agreement?

7 What did the Iraqis mean by 'a disguised form of annexation'?

12 Syrians fight the Mandate

In the nineteenth century France built up commercial links with the parts of the Ottoman Empire generally known as 'Syria'. French became widely spoken by merchants and traders. The secret Sykes–Picot agreement gave France a Syrian 'sphere of influence' which became a mandated territory.

The French government promised Syria a constitution and carried out road building and irrigation developments. But Syrian nationalists wanted independence. Opposition grew and the French dealt with it harshly. In October 1925 rebellion broke out in Damascus. Sources A and B provide written and photographic evidence of the disorders, in which 1416 civilians were said to have died. The Druze people (which can also be spelt Druse), a minority group of Muslims living mainly around Damascus and in the mountainous Jebel-el-Druse to the south, resisted for a further eighteen months. A widely-travelled Englishwoman, Freya Stark, writes from the Jebel-el-Druse in 1928 (Source C), describing the attitude of the French towards the locals.

A   Damascus, 1925

On the night of Saturday, October 17, French soldiers were attacked and mutilated in one of the low quarters . . . The next morning there appeared in the Shagour quarter a band of some threescore brigands, led by one Hassan al Kharrat, a former chief ghaffir* of the city . . . *nightwatchman*
A little later another band coming from a Druse village to the south of the city . . . appeared in the Meidan quarter. Both bands made for the bazaars and the centre of the city and started looting . . .

At midday on the 18th the French sent tanks through the city and these passed through the bazaars at a terrific speed, firing to the right and left without ceasing. The mob erected barricades in the rear of the tanks and when they were returning they were shot at from above, many of their crews being wounded . . .

The next morning, suddenly, and without warning all the troops were withdrawn from the old city, including the Christian quarters, and concentrated at Salaliyeh at which were the French cantonments*, *residential areas*
whither all French families were removed. From 10 o'clock for 24 hours the bombardment . . . was continued by artillery outside the city, while aeroplanes flew overhead dropping bombs and using machine-guns. Only at noon on the 20th did the firing cease . . .

I made an extensive tour of the city and was shocked at the havoc wrought in every direction. The whole area lying between the Hamadieh Bazaar and the Street Called Straight had been laid in ruins . . . the Great Mosque escaped . . . but not so the beautiful green and blue tiled Senaniyeh Mosque which has an enormous hole in the dome made by a shell . . .

From The Correspondent, *The Times*, 27 October 1925.

B Senaniyeh Mosque, shortly after 20 October 1925

C Letter from Jebel-el-Druse, 1928.

It is ridiculous to call this a mandate, for I believe there is not a Frenchman in the country who intends these people ever to govern themselves. It is their bad manners that annoy me so. They talk of them and to them as if they were scarce to be considered as human beings. If the Druses ever get a chance, they will not leave a man of them alive in the whole district . . .

From Freya Stark, *Letters from Syria*, John Murray, 1943.

Questions

1 Suggest why the French reacted so fiercely to the disorders.

2 What impression does *The Times* correspondent give of the Damascus rebels? How might a sympathetic journalist have described them?

3 Which parts of Source A seem based on what the journalist actually experienced? From whom might he have gathered the rest of his information?

4 What evidence do Sources A and B provide of French use of shells and bombs?

5 Why does Freya Stark say 'it is ridiculous to call this a mandate'?

6 How is a colony different from a mandate?

7 Give evidence from Sources A and B which support Freya Stark's views about French rule.

Part 3

Palestine 1920–49

13 A partition plan, 1937

Britain had two obligations as ruler of the Mandate in Palestine. The League of Nations expected her to bring the country to self-government, while Britain herself had promised the Zionists that Jews could build a national home there. A census taken in 1922 showed a population of 590,890 Muslim Arabs, 73,024 Christian Arabs and 83,794 Jews. Source A shows the figures for Jewish immigration and emigration from Palestine from then up to 1939.

The Arabs resisted Jewish settlement and Jewish purchase of Arab lands. From 1929 there were Arab attacks on Jewish property and in 1936 an Arab general strike brought most of Palestine's business and transport to a standstill. The British government set up a Royal Commission headed by Lord Peel which said that Arabs and Jews could never share power in the same state. It recommended a partition into two countries with Jerusalem staying under the Mandate (Source B). The Arabs refused to agree to this partition or to ones suggested later. Source C is from evidence against partition given by the Arab Office in Jerusalem in 1946.

A Jewish immigration and emigration, 1922–39

	1922	1923	1924	1925	1926	1927	1928	1929	1930
Immigration	7844	7421	12856	33801	13081	2713	2178	5249	4944
Emigration	1503	3466	*	2151	7365	5071	2168	1746	1679
	1931	1932	1933	1934	1935	1936	1937	1938	1939
Immigration	4075	9553	30327	42359	61854	29727	10536	12868	16405
Emigration	666	**	**	**	396	773	889	1095	1019

From Esco Foundation, *Palestine, a study of Jewish, Arab and British Policies*, Yale University Press, 1947.

*figures incomplete
**figures not reported

B Peel Commission, 1937

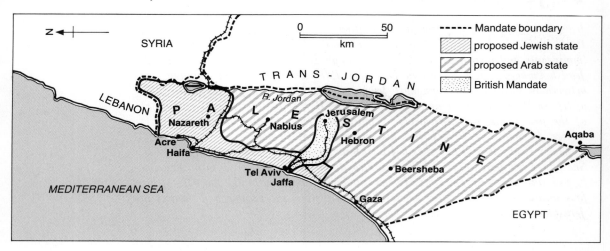

C An Arab view of partition

The idea of partition and the establishment of a Jewish state in a part of Palestine is inadmissible for the same reasons of principle as the idea of establishing a Jewish state in the whole country. If it is unjust to the Arabs to impose a Jewish state on the whole of Palestine, it is equally unjust to impose it in any part of the country. Moreover . . . there are grave difficulties in the way of partition; commerce would be strangled, communications dislocated and the public finances upset. It would also be impossible to devise frontiers which would not leave a large Arab minority in the Jewish state. Moreover partition would not satisfy the Zionists . . .

From W. Laqueur and B. Rubin (eds.), *The Israel-Arab Reader* (4th Edition), Facts on File Publications, 1985.

Questions

1 Use Source A to construct a graph of immigration.

2 What might explain a) variations in immigration and emigration figures, 1925–28, b) the rise in immigration 1932–35, c) the fall in immigration from 1936, and d) the emigration rates for the 1930s?

3 Why might historians treat with caution the figures in Source A?

4 As a member of the Peel Commission how would you have explained the partition boundaries and the creation of a new British mandate zone?

5 How did the Arab Office justify its opposition to partition or a Jewish state? What evidence is there in Sources A and B to back Arab arguments?

14 Jewish settlers

Jews who had fled the violent persecutions in Russia during 1881–82 and 1904–1905 were known as halutzim, or pioneers. They became the most respected immigrants amongst Jews in Palestine. Joseph Baratz, the son of a Ukrainian Jewish innkeeper, left Russia in December 1906 when he was only sixteen. He believed in social equality amongst Jews and wished to help pioneer a new way of life in Palestine. Arriving at Jaffa by ship, Baratz and his friends visited one of the first immigrant settlements, founded at Rishon-le-Zion twenty five years earlier. In Source A, he describes his impressions of Rishon.

Molly Lyons Bar-David was a Jewish immigrant from Canada in April 1936. She joined her parents, who had emigrated the previous year, on a farm they had helped start north of Tel Aviv. In her autobiography (Source B) she tells of her first impressions of the farm where she worked until she became a journalist in Jerusalem a few years later.

A Visit to Rishon-le-Zion, 1906

The country looked very different from what it is today. Now, next to Jaffa there is Tel Aviv and beyond it all the valley is dark green with orange groves; but in those days you walked straight into sand dunes; it was sad country, like a desert all the way until you came to the plantations of Rishon.

Naturally we were excited when we saw them – in a moment we would see a Jewish village. But we thought that to talk with the Biluim* we would have to wait until sunset – we imagined a village like in Russia – hens pecking in the road, children shouting by the river, and not a soul in sight while the sun is high and all the peasants are in the fields.

But what is this? We were in a pretty street of neat brick houses with red tiled roofs; from one of them came the tinkling of a piano. The street was full of people strolling up and down. We couldn't believe our eyes. We asked:
'Who are these?'
'Biluim.'
'And who does the work?'
'Arabs.'
'And what do the Jews do?'
'They're managers, supervisors.'
It was a great shock to us. I said to myself; 'This isn't what I've come for,' and I could see that the others were disappointed as well.

From Joseph Baratz, *A Village by the Jordan*, Harvill Press, 1954.

earliest group of Jewish immigrants

B Gan Hasharon, 1936

Our shoes oozing with sand, we approached the gate to Gan Hasharon. This was incredible. Afloat in a sea of sand was a stretch of fenced-in oasis. The massive wrought-iron gate bore: 'Gan Hasharon' spelled out in Hebrew letters, and its pillars were smothered in purple bougainvillea. We entered a long avenue of giant trees greeting us with the chirping of a thousand birds. We followed along this dark cathedral aisle of trees and entered an avenue of cypress, forming a green wall with spires. We stood on the hilltop and marvelled. The propaganda we heard aboard was all true ... The Sahara could not have looked more forbidding than the field over the road where an old Bedouin was trying to eke out a living by growing a few watermelons. On our side, in an equal area, a group of Canadian Jews from Saskatoon, with Dad among them, had planted an orange grove. They had dug for water – the first in the district – installed a diesel engine, irrigated the soil, and no fewer than three hundred souls* made a good living out of the stretch of land. And to see it! Or rather to smell it! The waxen orange blossoms were peeping out of the shiny leaves. The perfume is something I have never got used to: love and romance and adventure in ethereal* form ...

The first thing that greeted us when we entered the little hut my parents were living in was a steel box with 'Gan Hasharon – 6' stamped on it. 'These are our guns,' said Dad. 'The Government gave this colony six of them after the unhappy incident of 1929. Our watchmen have extra rifles and this box hasn't been opened yet.' A week later that box was unsealed.

From Molly Lyons Bar-David, *My Promised Land*, G. P. Putnam's Sons, 1953

* *some were Arabs*

* *heavenly*

Questions

1 In which ways was Rishon different from a Russian village?

2 Explain what Baratz meant when he thought: 'This isn't what I've come for'.

3 What did the author of Source B think was 'true' about the 'propaganda' she had heard on her way to Palestine?

4 Explain the meaning of the sentence in Source B 'The perfume is something ... ethereal form'.

5 Suggest the dangers hinted at in the final paragraph of Source B.

6 What clue can be found, in both sources, to the most important difficulty farmers had to face when they started at Rishon and Gan Hasharon?

7 As if in the mid-1930s, either write a short piece for a British newspaper which you hope will attract Jewish immigrants to Palestine, or design a poster which an Arab group might display to protest about immigration.

15 Arab resistance

Arab riots against Jews broke out in 1919 and 1921. The British governor of Palestine, a Jew, tried to cool Arab tempers in May 1921 by appointing a popular Muslim leader, Haj Amin al-Husseini as Grand Mufti of Jerusalem. Tension mounted again in 1929 with Zionist demonstrations and fiery speeches by Haj Amin. In August there were Arab attacks on Jews. Source A is from a British newspaper which gave Jewish eye-witness accounts of events at Hebron where 64 Jews died. Source B is from an article in an Arab newspaper four years later. In April 1936 there was a general strike of Arab workers, described in Source C which is taken from a letter by a young British official.

In 1937, Haj Amin and Arab leaders rejected the Peel plan for partition and organised a revolt which took the British two years to put down. They exiled Haj Amin from Palestine. In 1941 he declared a jihad, *or holy war, against Britain and went to Berlin to enlist Hitler's support (Source D). Haj Amin went back to the Middle East after the war, but never returned to Palestine.*

A Jewish eye-witnesses

Chief Rabbi Slonim . . . said: A band of Arabs broke into the Talmudic College, killing one student. Other students escaped to the cellars of a neighbouring house. Taking our lives in our hands, I and my friends went to see the chief of police. He refused to see us. On Saturday morning the Arabs broke into our house. A friendly Arab stood in front of me to protect me and swore he would be killed himself rather than that I should be harmed.

A student said: Those in the house of the rabbi's son barred their doors, took hold of Bibles and holy books and recited psalms and hymns. Yelling, the Arabs smashed their way into the house with axes and iron bars. Eighteen of those in the house were killed . . . The Arab police stood by while the massacre continued. Then the Arabs began looting and the reign of terror lasted until next day when armed British police arrived. They ended the rioting by shooting thirty of the Arabs on the spot.

From the London *Daily Mail*, 30 August 1929.

B A Palestinian Arab remembers

Today is the anniversary of the August uprising . . . the flames of which were borne high on this day in 1929. That day was a day of brilliance and glory in the annals of Palestinian–Arab history. This is the day of honour, splendour and sacrifice. We attacked Western conquest and the Mandate and the Zionists upon our land. The Jews have coveted our endowments and yearned to take over our holy places. In our silence they had seen a sign of weakness, therefore there was no more room in our hearts for patience or peace; no sooner had the Jews begun marching along this shameful road than the Arabs stood up, checked the oppression, and sacrificed their pure and noble souls on the sacred altar of nationalism.

From Y. Porath, *The Emergence of the Palestinian–Arab nationalist movement, 1918–1929*, Frank Cass, 1974.

C A British official's view

For the present it seems as if the killing of Jews by Arabs and of Arabs by police has left off, which is a comfort, and the unrest has taken the form of what looks as if it may become a prolonged general strike among Arabs. That is a better way of putting pressure on the Government, I think, though it is bound to involve a lot of suffering for the workers and shopkeepers who strike. At present the strike is not complete. Most of the Arab shops all over the country are shut, except foodshops, restaurants and cafes. The port is working here, but at Jaffa I think work has stopped. The railways are still working, but there isn't much road communication between the large towns – Jewish cars and lorries move mostly under convoy.

From E. C. Hodgkin (ed.), Thomas Hodgkin, *Letters from Palestine, 1932–6*, Quartet Books, 1986.

D The Grand Mufti and the Führer, Berlin 1941

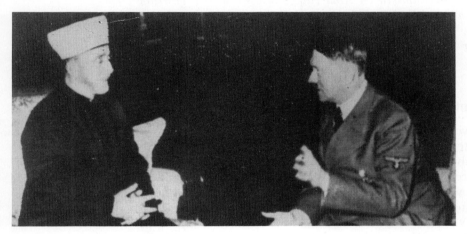

Questions

1 What do you learn from Source A of Arab attitudes towards Jews in Hebron?

2 Why does the author of Source B write of a 'day of honour, splendour and sacrifice'? If he had added to his remarks, which facts from A might he have included or omitted?

3 Does the writer in Source C say anything to suggest he sympathises with the strike?

4 What evidence do A and C and Source A in Unit 16 provide of British willingness to protect Jews from Arab attacks?

5 From B and C, and Source A in Unit 13, suggest why the Arabs resisted the British Mandate.

6 Suggest why the Grand Mufti went to Adolf Hitler for help. What impact would the photograph have had on his opponents?

16 Haganah

In 1920, a secret Jewish defence force called Haganah was formed in Palestine after Arab attacks in March and April caused the deaths of 47 Jews. Membership shot up when more Arab rioting in 1929 and 1936 resulted in many more Jewish deaths. In Source A, Molly Bar-David describes how she joined a Haganah unit in 1936 when her farm was frequently attacked by Arab guerrillas. The photograph shows the type of defences that Jewish immigrants put up to protect settlements, such as this one near the Lebanese border.

In 1936, members of Haganah wanted to change the policy of havlaga, *or self-restraint, so they could go on the offensive against Arab guerrilla targets. Co-operation between Haganah and the police, mentioned in Source A, went further as Haganah volunteers joined special police units known as Night Squads. In Source B, a former commander of a Haganah mobile unit recalls in a television interview how the Haganah attacked an Arab village thought to be a guerrilla base. A few Haganah members joined the rival extremist organization, Irgun, (see Unit 17) which, unlike Haganah, launched indiscriminate attacks on the Arab population after 1936.*

A Training for defence

My sister and I were invited to join the Hagana, the Jewish secret militia. We met after dark one night in an orange packing shed in the middle of a neighbouring grove; the whole atmosphere was one of conspiracy and unreality. Discipline and democracy rubbed shoulders in a most unusual way. We called our commander by his first name, argued with him often enough, but obeyed him without a quibble when we got an order. We were taught in the use of such mild weapons as revolvers and shotguns. We also learned first aid, signalling and the rules of the game . . . Everyone learned to use a weapon, but our arms were defence arms only. For the Hagana, which means 'defence', had been instructed by the Jewish governing bodies to shoot only if shot at and to shoot only from one's threshold. The police and the Hagana often came to each other's defence.

From Molly Lyons Bar-David, *My Promised Land*, G. P. Putnam's Sons, 1953.

B Going on the offensive

Yitzhak Sadeh went out to Kalandiya, without me. He sought some way of not having to attack the village and yet to reach the people. The farthest-range weapons he could find were grenade rifles. That's what we had in the Hagana. Every platoon was issued with just one such grenade rifle with ten grenades. That was all. He gathered twelve rifles and twelve men and after some training, all twelve aimed at the village. He said, 'boom, boom', and there were twelve times ten explosions. After that Kalandiya became quiet.

From Yigal Lossin, *Pillar of Fire*, Shikmona Publishing Company Ltd., 1983.

C Tower and stockade, 1938

Questions

1 Does the photograph suggest that the siting of the settlement made it vulnerable to attack?

2 List the weapons and fortifications in Sources A and C that would protect settlers against attack.

3 What does Bar-David mean by 'the rules of the game'?

4 Is there anything in Source A which suggests why Haganah was formed?

5 In what ways did Sadeh seem to go further than he intended in the attack on Kalandiya? What does the former Haganah man really mean when he says 'Kalandiya became quiet'?

6 Using Sources A and B above, and Source C in Unit 15, explain the change in the Haganah's principle of *havlaga* during the 1930s.

17 The King David Hotel, July 1946

In 1931 a Russian Zionist, Vladimir Jabotinsky, founded the Irgun Zvai Leumi or National Military Organisation. Jabotinsky and the Irgun set out to challenge the members of the Jewish Agency, who were recognised by most Jews in Palestine as their leaders. The Agency controlled the Haganah, and for most of the time limited it to armed defence agaist Arabs while the Irgun organised terror and violence against them. In 1944 the Irgun had a new leader, Menachem Begin, a Polish Zionist who had come to Palestine in 1942 with bitter memories of anti-semitism in Europe. Begin saw Britain as a greater obstacle to a Jewish state than the Arabs and launched an armed campaign against her rule. The Irgun openly criticised the Jewish Agency in posters which were put up in Palestine in 1945 and 1946 (Source A).

Such pressure led to the Haganah co-operating with the Irgun and another terrorist group, the Stern Gang, between November 1945 and July 1946. All three agreed to an Irgun attack on the King David Hotel which housed the British headquarters in Jerusalem. Source B, taken from the memoirs of Menachem Begin, describes how the attack was planned. At 12.37 pm on 22 July 1946 the hotel's west wing was destroyed. Ninety-one people died, including 41 Arabs, 28 Britons and 17 Jews. Source C is from an Irgun poster pasted on walls the day after. Source D is a statement from the Jewish Agency and other political leaders.

A   The Irgun on the Agency

"I WANT TO LIVE"   "I WANT TO LIVE"

The Fighting, Hebrew Resistance Way

The Submissive, Jewish Agency Way

B Begin's plan of attack

A prime consideration was the timing of the attack. Two proposals were made: one for eleven am, the other for between four and five o'clock in the afternoon . . . In these morning and afternoon hours the Cafe was usually empty. At lunchtime it was filled with customers . . . civilian men and women as well as Army officers. It was essential that the attack be delivered at an hour when there were no customers in the Cafe . . .

Because of last minute consultations, the time of the attack was delayed by one hour and began at twelve o'clock instead of eleven.

From M. Begin, *The Revolt*, Steimatzky's Agency Ltd., 1951.

C The Irgun statement

Yesterday at 12.05 pm soldiers of the Irgun Zvai Leumi attacked the central building of the British power of occupation in Palestine. Before the attack the bombs were placed so as to explode half an hour later. Immediately after that the telephone operator of the K.D.*, several newspapers, agencies, and the French consulate were warned by telephone. Also a little alarm bomb which could do no harm was placed before the K.D. and exploded so that the hotel could be evacuated in time. The tragedy which happened in the offices of the Government is not the guilt of the Jewish soldiers who have received orders to spare lives . . . The warnings by telephone were given between 12.10 and 12.15 so that the British had 22 minutes to evacuate the building and therefore the whole responsibility falls on the British . . .

From T. Clarke, *By Blood and Fire*, G. P. Putnam's Sons, 1981.

* *King David Hotel*

D The Agency's statement

The Executive of the Jewish Agency and the Executive of the Vaad Leumi* express their horror at the dastardly crime perpetrated by the gang of desperadoes who today attacked the Government offices in Jerusalem, and shed the innocent blood of Government officers and other citizens, British, Jewish and Arab.

From the *Palestine Post*, Jerusalem, 23 July 1946.

* *the 'National Council' of Jews*

Questions

1 In your own words explain the message of the posters.

2 In which ways do Sources B and C agree and disagree about the timing of the attack?

3 How does Irgun in Source C justify putting 'the whole responsibility' on the British?

4 Why do you think they needed to blame the British?

5 Why did the Agency put out the statement (D), even though the Irgun had said the casualties were not their fault?

6 Imagine British officials in Palestine reading Source B. How do you think they would have reacted?

18 Britain decides to withdraw, 1947

After winning the general election in July 1945 the new Labour Government said it would work for a single independent Palestine. The Arabs would remain in the majority because the British government would limit the immigration of Jews. The government's policy led the Jewish Agency to agree secretly to a combined guerrilla campaign by the Haganah, Irgun and Stern groups against British rule.

After the first wave of guerrilla attacks the British Foreign Secretary, Ernest Bevin, met the London representatives of the Jewish Agency. Source A, from a biography of Ernest Bevin, is an account of what he told them. By February 1947, Palestine had become so difficult to administer that the British government told the UN that it would hand the mandate back to them. Jewish guerrilla violence continued. Source C shows the reaction of the Daily Express *to the Irgun's killing of two British soldiers in retaliation for the trial and execution of two of their members.*

In Source B Sir Harold Beeley, a senior British diplomat, remembers Bevin's policy in 1947 towards the Middle East.

A Ernest Bevin on terrorism, November 1945

Bevin summoned Weizmann and Moshe Shertok to see him. The latter's account describes Bevin as speaking with 'great anger and tension, a muscle at the side of his mouth giving a warning signal'. He laid stress on the cooperation between the Haganah and the terrorist organizations; saying that this amounted to a declaration of war . . . 'I cannot bear English Tommies being killed. They are innocent.' When Weizmann referred to the millions of Jews who had been killed and were still dying in refugee camps, Bevin replied: 'I do not want any Jews killed either, but I love the British soldiers. They belong to my class. They are working people.'

Shertok noted that 'Bevin's anger and fury against the United States are unimaginable.' As an example of American dishonesty he cited Truman's claim 'for electoral purposes for the immediate entry of 100,000 – a course which the President and everyone else who understood the problem knew was impossible today'.

From A. Bullock, *Ernest Bevin, Foreign Secretary*, O.U.P., 1983.

B A diplomat's assessment

All through 1947, Bevin was negotiating with prime ministers Nokrashi and Saleh Jabr of Egypt and Iraq, for the protection of the Suez Canal and our oil concessions, and to integrate the two countries into the Western alliance. All this would have been ruined if we had played a part in creating the state of Israel.

From Conor Cruise O'Brien, *The Siege*, Weidenfeld and Nicolson, 1986.

36

C

Pinned to the body on the right is a notice: 'This is the sentence of Irgun's High Tribunal'. The ground under one of the bodies was booby-trapped.

Questions

1 In Source A, what accusation does Bevin make against a) Weizmann and Shertok, and b) the U.S. President?

2 Can you explain Bevin's feelings about the deaths of Jews and Tommies?

3 In which ways might 'the immediate entry of 100,000 Jews' have caused difficulties?

4 How might the *Daily Express* report have affected British public opinion? Could the newspaper be criticized for presenting the news this way?

5 What evidence is there in the news that Britain was still feeling the effects of the Second World War? Would this have any influence on views about Palestine?

6 According to Beeley (B), why was it impossible for Britain to be both friendly towards Arab states and help to create Israel?

7 Describe in your own words how Britain's position in Palestine had become 'intolerably difficult' by the end of 1947.

19 The *Exodus*, July 1947

The British allowed 1500 Jewish refugees into Palestine every month. They turned others back or put them into internment camps. In July 1947, 4500 concentration camp survivors set sail from France in a river steamer which the Haganah bought in America and renamed the Exodus. *Five British warships shadowed her to the eastern Mediterranean and then sent boarding parties who fought with the refugees, killing three and wounding 28 seriously. The ship docked at Haifa. Photographs of its condition and a statement from its crew were printed in newspapers around the world (Sources A and B). The British sent the uninjured back to France. In France, they refused to land, so the British Foreign Secretary, Ernest Bevin, ordered them to be taken to a displaced persons camp in Germany. One Jewish group turned this into a chance for propaganda (Source C). Source D is from an interview given by the* Exodus *captain to an historian some years later.*

A The ship, 18 July 1947

B The crew's statement

In the battle lasting two hours, our ship was rammed, constantly bombed with tear gas, sprayed with water from high-pressure hoses and fired at with pistols and sub-machine guns. Our resistance continued without let-up . . . Only when the ship's commander was informed that the wounded were coming into the ship's hospital at a rate too great to be treated, did he give the order to cease resistance and avoid a large loss of life . . .

From the *New York Herald Tribune*, 21 July 1947.

D The captain's interview, 1970s

Mossad le-Aliya* not only suggested, they gave us orders that this ship was to be used as a big demonstration with banners to show how poor and weak and helpless we were, and how cruel the British were. I was told to make as much of a demonstration as possible, but not to let the fight go too far.

* Haganah's refugee section

From Nicholas Bethell, *The Palestine Triangle*, André Deutsch, 1979.

Questions

1 How much evidence is there in Source A of damage to the *Exodus*?

2 How reliable do you think the crew's statement is? In which ways might it be exaggerated?

3 Did Bevin's treatment of the refugees give the 'flag' (Source C) any particular meaning?

4 How do Sources B and D a) agree, and b) disagree?

5 Can the captain's statement be used as proof that the fight was only a propaganda exercise?

6 What would have been the effect of Sources A, B and C on newspaper readers in a) the United States, and b) Britain?

7 If the *Exodus* operation was partly a propaganda exercise, do you think it was justified?

20 The Arabs leave, 1948

Before the end of the British mandate on 14 May 1948, Jewish and Arab guerrillas fought to control western and northern Palestine and the road linking Tel Aviv with Jerusalem. There were heavy civilian casualties. On 9 April the Irgun killed 250 Arab men, women and children at Deir Yassin. In reprisal, Arab guerrillas killed 77 Jewish civilians, including doctors and patients, in an ambush within sight of Jerusalem.

300,000 Arabs fled their homes even before Israel was declared. Later there were bitter disagreements about the flight which left the Jews holding so much Arab property and forming a very clear majority in Israel. Were the Arabs forced out? Did they leave out of panic? Did Arab leaders encourage them to leave? Two of the largest groups fled from Haifa and Jaffa, captured by the Haganah on 22 April and 12 May. The chief operations officer of the Haganah and a member of the Arab National Committee give their accounts of the flight from Haifa in Sources A and B. A former British army commander describes events in Jaffa in Source C, and D shows the town at the time. In Source E a Haganah commander explains the flight of Arabs from Galilee.

A Haifa: Yigael Yadin

. . . I can testify personally that superhuman efforts were made, in defiance of logic, one could say, on the part of the Haganah Command, the District Command and the political leadership to try and keep the Arabs from leaving . . . Not Deir Yassin itself, but the character of the Arab propaganda which exploited the incident at Deir Yassin influenced the Arabs to flee . . . The way in which the Arabs exploited Deir Yassin, I would say, was the boomerang which hurt them most.

From Yigal Lossin, *Pillar of Fire*, Shikmona Publishing Company Ltd., 1983.

B Haifa: Farid Sa'ad

. . . Sa'ad said that no order had been given to the Arab population telling them to leave. He said that those members of the National Committee who remained in Haifa were telling people to use their own judgement as to whether they should stay or leave. People were in a panic after the unexpectedly easy Jewish victory. Subsequent Jewish looting and attacks on refugees had simply added to the panic.

From Michael Palumbo, *The Palestinian Catastrophe*, Faber and Faber, 1987.

C Jaffa: General Sir Horatius Murray

There I saw a scene which I never thought to see in my life . . . all the people of Jaffa, pouring out on to the road carrying in the hands whatever they could pick up, awfully well dressed people – women, children, men. No transport. They were heading South as fast as their legs could carry them and it was a case of sheer terror. It was just as if the Pied Piper had been there. There wasn't a soul. Gas stoves were still burning in the houses.

From R. Broad, *Palestine* (film transcript), Thames Television, 1978.

D Jaffa: refugees leave, May 1947

E Galilee: Yigal Allon

I gathered all the Jewish Mayors who had contact with the Arabs in different villages and asked them to whisper in the ears of some Arabs that great Jewish reinforcements had arrived in Galilee and that they were going to burn all the villages in the Hula valley. They should suggest to these Arabs as their friends that it was best for them to escape while there was still time. Thus the rumour spread in all parts of the Hula valley that it was time to flee. There was a massive exodus.

From Michael Palumbo, *The Palestinian Catastrophe*, Faber and Faber, 1987.

Questions

1 What does Yigael Yadin mean by saying Jewish commanders acted in 'defiance of logic'?

2 Compare the reasons given for the flight from Haifa in A and B. Is there any reason to believe one more than the other? Does Murray's account of the flight from Jaffa match either?

3 How do C and D agree?

4 What were the main differences between Arabs in Jaffa and Galilee?

5 How far does Yigal Allon's explanation support or conflict with the other sources?

6 Use the sources to write a discussion between two Palestinian refugees about why they left and whether they had been right to do so.

21 Partition, 1949

The state of Israel was declared on 14 May 1948, but no Arab state recognised her. In Source A, David Ben Gurion talks to his military commanders about Israel's defence. On 15 May, Syria entered the Jordan valley, Iraqi forces and the Jordanian Arab Legion moved west across the River Jordan and the Egyptian army attacked north towards Tel Aviv. Fierce Israeli resistance halted the advances. The United Nations Security Council arranged truces from 11 June to 8 July and between 18 July and October. Source B is from the memoirs of an Egyptian commander, Mohammad Naguib, who recalls the condition of Egypt's forces in July. The Arab Legion's British commander, General Glubb, recalls his difficulties (Source C). In October Israel drove the Egyptian forces out of the Negev. In January 1949, Israel signed separate armistices with Egypt, Lebanon, Jordan and Syria. The map shows how the war increased Israel's boundaries beyond those proposed by the UN.

A   Ben Gurion, May 1948

The three places we must defend with the greatest vigour . . . are Tel Aviv, Haifa and Jerusalem. If we lose Tel Aviv, we can establish a bridgehead in Haifa. If we lose Haifa, the major part of our national strength will still be intact in Tel Aviv. But if we lose Jerusalem, the blow to our morale will be so great that I cannot visualize we could keep Tel Aviv and Haifa.

From D. Kurzman, *Genesis 1948*, Vallentine, Mitchell and Co. Ltd., 1970.

B   An Egyptian view

Between truces we fought as well as we could with the limited amounts of poor equipment at our disposal. Many of our British guns and mortars could not be used for lack of shells. Many of our American tanks were crippled for lack of spare parts . . . The rifles we received from Spain were Mausers dating from 1912. They were all right for training purposes, but they were of little use against the automatic Czech, Russian and American weapons with which the enemy was supplied.

From Mohammed Naguib, *Egypt's Destiny*, Doubleday and Company, 1955.

C   J. B. Glubb, Arab Legion commander

The truce was due to end on 11 July. The Arab armies were in no position to renew hostilities. Only Egypt and Jordan were in close contact with the Israelis, and neither had any reserve ammunition or any outside source of supply. Both armies had originally been equipped by Britain, who was conscientiously applying the ruling of the Security Council and refused to supply them with any war-like stores . . .

'But how can we continue to fight without ammunition?' I asked the Prime Minister.*

'Don't shoot unless the Jews shoot first,' he replied.

From J. B. Glubb, *The Changing Scenes of Life*, Quartet Books, 1983.

* of Jordan

D   Israel and her neighbours, 1949

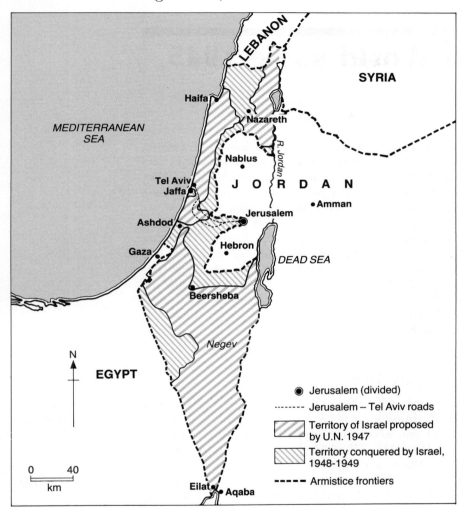

Questions

1 Why does Ben Gurion say that the loss of Jerusalem would be such a great 'blow to our morale'?

2 Use Sources B and C to explain the differences in arms between the two sides. What reasons for them are given in the sources?

3 Why did each Arab country agree only to an armistice with Israel?

4 How might a Palestinian have answered a journalist's question in July 1949: 'What are your views on the outcome of the recent conflict?'?

Part 4

The Arab World since 1945

22 Nasser

Gamal Abdel Nasser was born in 1918, the son of a postal official in Alexandria. As an army officer he joined the secret Free Officers movement of nationalists who aimed to free Egypt from Western domination and end the corrupt rule of King Farouk. By 1952, Nasser was a colonel and in July he took part in an army coup led by General Naguib which forced Farouk into exile. The following year Nasser became deputy prime minister in a military government which banned all political parties. In April 1954 he ousted Naguib and took over as Prime Minister. In June 1956 he became President. The photograph shows some of the 50,000 who heard Nasser speak in Manshiyeh Square in Alexandria on the evening of 26 July 1956. A week earlier the United States had told Nasser they would not give aid for the Nile Dam he planned at Aswan. Nasser used his speech to send a coded message and then make an important announcement. A French journalist who was present recalls that evening in his biography of Nasser.

A Nasser's speech, 26 July 1956

He spoke in a familiar tone, what Egyptians call *baladi*, the popular language, this time not straining for a noble style as he had done before . . . 'And now I shall tell you about my unpleasant dealings with the American diplomats . . . Poor Mr. Allen! He comes into my office with the note – I drive him out; he returns without having delivered the note – Mr. Dulles* drives him out. What can be done for poor Mr. Allen?'

Suddenly the tone changed. An ironic description of his last meeting with Mr. Black* brought the *Rais*** to the sentence awaited by the teams lying in wait along the canal, transistor in hand, at Port Said, Ismailia, and Suez: 'This gentleman reminded me of Ferdinand de Lesseps'* (pronounced 'Lissips' with a hiss) . . . Then the crescendo: 'We are going to take back the profits which this imperialist company, this state within a state, deprived us while we were dying of hunger . . .'

So that was it! 'I announced to you that at this very moment our official newspaper is publishing the law nationalizing the company, and, as I speak to you, government agents are taking possession of the company . . .'. Everything exploded around and below us in the darkness. Newspapermen known for their scepticism toward the regime climbed onto their chairs to roar their enthusiasm.

Gamal was suddenly shaken by an irrepressible laugh: the thrill was enormous, the move surprising even to him. He shouted his defiance:

From Jean Lacouture, *Nasser*, Secker and Warburg, 1973.

* *American Secretary of State*

* *President of the World Bank*
**leader*
* *Frenchman who built the Suez Canal*

'The canal will pay for the dam! Four years ago, in this very place, Farouk fled Egypt. Today I seize the canal, in the name of the people ... This night our canal shall be Egyptian, controlled by Egyptians!'

B Manshiyeh Square, Alexandria, 26 July 1956

Questions

1 Which past event was the rally in Manshiyeh Square being held to commemorate?

2 Is there evidence in the photograph that the organisers were worried about Nasser's safety?

3 Which phrase in Nasser's speech were men with transistors waiting for? What did they do when they heard it?

4 Write down words Nasser used in his speech that suggest he was a) a nationalist, and b) a socialist.

5 What propagandist techniques were used to publicize the Manshiyeh Square rally?

6 If you had been an Egyptian at the rally, how would you have described the occasion in a letter to a friend afterwards?

7 How might a British diplomat, also present that evening, have reported to London on Nasser's speech and the rally?

45

23 Suez Crisis

In July 1954 Britain withdrew her troops from the Suez Canal Zone, keeping the right to return if the Canal were threatened by a non-Arab country. Egypt's relations with Western powers worsened from December 1955 when Nasser ordered arms from communist Czechoslovakia. On 19 July 1956 the USA withdrew her promise of finance for the dam at Aswan and Britain's prime minister Anthony Eden did the same. Nasser decided to nationalise the Canal Company which was mostly French and British owned. He discussed this in a secret telephone call to his close friend Mohammad Heikal, editor of a government-controlled newspaper. Source A is from Heikal's book about Nasser in which he reconstructs the plan which Nasser called 'If I were Eden'.

On 26 July 1956, Nasser nationalised the Company. On 24 October 1956, Britain, France and Israel secretly agreed to force Nasser to back down. The Israelis invaded Egypt a few days later. Britain and France issued an ultimatum to both sides to withdraw 16 kilometres from the Canal. Egypt refused and an Anglo–French invasion followed. The map shows details of the campaigns before the ceasefire on 7 November.

A If I were Eden

1 Eden will behave in a violent way.
2 The violence will take the form of military action. He will be violent because his position is weak. Violence is not strength. What can he do? A full invasion? Unlikely. Maybe he will try to force his way through the Suez Canal, by getting battleships into the Canal ... I can get a convoy taken in the other direction and meet them face to face so that they will block the Canal ...
3 The possibility of violence will be 80%. It depends on how many troops the British have ready for quick intervention from the Mediterranean, Aden, Cyprus or Malta.
4 Most probably Eden will try to pull France with him, or maybe France is going to pull Eden. But certainly France may participate in any operation against us.
5 The United States will remain silent, giving their blessing under the table ...
6 The position of Russia will be decisive ... Better not tell them. Estimate of their position: direct intervention in the case of invasion? Out of the question. Political support? Yes ...
8 Possibilities of the success of intervention ... Could they attack Alexandria via Libya? That would need big forces because they would be obliged to carry on to Cairo. Could they bombard Alexandria from the sea ...? Completely impossible. Landing, occupying the Canal? Possible. We need to reinforce Eastern Command.
9 Evacuation of Sinai ... Keep only necessary troops.
10 Israel. Participation of Israel in this operation to be ruled out. Eden would not accept. Israel may try but Eden will refuse. He will prefer to keep it European ...

From M. Heikal, *Nasser, The Cairo Documents,* New English Library, 1972.

B The Suez Campaign, October–November 1956

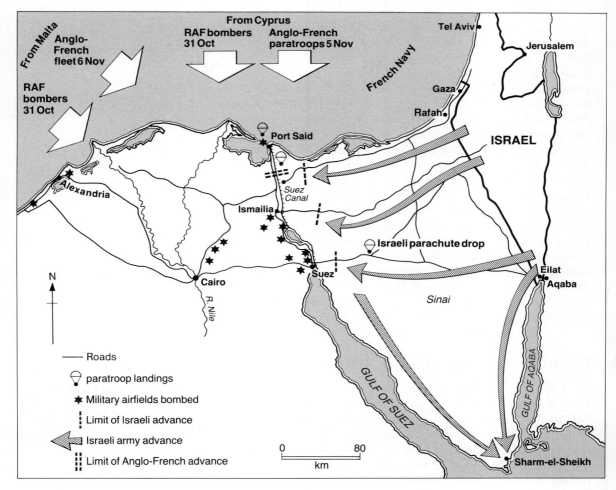

Questions

1 What did Nasser mean when he said 'Eden will behave in a violent way . . . because his position is weak'?

2 What did Nasser think the Americans and Russians would do? Can you suggest why Nasser thought this?

3 What does the map tell you about British and French military operations in October and November 1956?

How close were they to Nasser's forecast?

4 How did Nasser prevent ships from using the Canal during the war?

5 List the ways in which Nasser was a) right, and b) wrong about British, French and Israeli reactions to the nationalization of the Suez Canal Company.

24 Iraq army coup, 1958

Iraq gained her independence in June 1930 when King Faisal I signed a treaty that ended British rule under the League of Nations' Mandate. Soon after, Faisal died. His son, the play-boy King Ghazi, died in a car crash in April 1939, leaving the four year old Faisal II as king. In April 1941, Rashid Ali, a former prime minister, and four nationalist army officers, known as the 'Golden Square' who had links with Nazi Germany, led an overthrow of the government. A British force landed at Basra and quickly defeated the nationalists. Rashid Ali went into exile and many years later returned to Iraq as a hero.

Support for nationalism grew among Iraqis who resented Britain's share in the Iraq Petroleum Company and the British Air Force bases in the country. In 1955 the Prime Minister, Nuri as-Said signed the Baghdad Pact with Britain, Iran and Pakistan. Nationalists in Iraq and other Arab countries denounced this siding with the West. In 1958 with the secret support of Egypt, a group of nationalist army officers, led by Brigadier-General Qassem, plotted to overthrow Faisal II and his government. On the night of 13 July Iraq army units, ordered to move to the frontier with Jordan, entered Baghdad instead. Source A is an historian's account of what happened the next morning. Source B is from a proclamation read over Baghdad Radio by Qassem's second-in-command, Colonel Aref. Five years later, Qassem was overthrown. He was put on trial and shot. Colonel Aref and the Ba'ath party came to power.

A Brigadier-General Qassem's coup, 14 July 1958

At 4.30 am ... the brigade entered Baghdad. Colonel ad-Darraji's First Battalion rolled at once into ar-Rasafah on the east bank, and had to take possession of the administrative high points, including the Ministry of Defence. The Second Battalion ... had to neutralize the mobile police center ... and wrest its munitions depot. Aref's own battalion ... had to seize the radio station, Nuri's house, and the royal palace. Simultaneously, several officers' groups, guided directly by the Committee-in-Reserve of the Free Officers ... moved, as agreed upon beforehand, to occupy ar-Rashid camp and round up the chief of staff and other brass-hats.

Everything fell out as planned except for the escape of Nuri as-Said. It would also appear that the shooting down of the royal family in the palace grounds was not premeditated ...

At about 7.45 am, after a brief parley of its commander with emissaries of the besiegers, the Royal Guard surrendered. A little before 8.00, the king*, the prince**, and other members of the royal household stumbled out the back entrance of the palace into the courtyard to face half a circle of officers. Moments later, from the front entrance emerged at a run, a submachine gun in his hand, Captain Abd-us-Sattar Sab al-Abusi, one of the emissaries, who, instantly and from behind, fired into the royal family. His action touched off a burst of bullets from every direction and from everyone bearing arms. Not only did the king and

From Hanna Batatu, *The Old Social Classes and the Revolutionary Movements of Iraq*, Princeton University Press, 1978.

* Faisal II
**Crown Prince Abdul Illah

his party fall to the ground, but also three of the officers that had stood in the semicircle . . .

As for Nuri as-Said, he was, as is known, caught the next day disguised as a woman, and was at once done to death by an air force sergeant. His body was, after burial, disinterred by an angry crowd and, like that of the intensely hated crown prince, dragged through the streets, strung up, torn to pieces, and finally burnt. Inhumaneness? It is perhaps not appropriate to pass judgment but it must be added, not to justify but to explain, that Nuri and the prince were never tender with the lives of their people. And then is it very strange that inhumaneness should issue from the dehumanizing conditions in which the . . . mud hutters of Baghdad subsisted?

B Proclamation No. 1, 6.30 am, 14 July 1958

Noble people of Iraq,

Trusting in God and with the aid of the loyal sons of the people and the national armed forces, we have undertaken to liberate the beloved homeland from the corrupt crew that imperialism installed . . .

Brethren,

The army is of you and for you and has carried out what you desired . . . Your duty is to support it . . . in the wrath that it is pouring on the Rihab Palace and the house of Nuri as-Said. Only by preserving it from the plots of imperialism and its stooges can victory be brought to completion. We appeal to you . . . to report to the authorities all offenders, traitors, and corrupt people so that they could be uprooted . . .

O People,

We have taken oath to sacrifice our blood and everything we hold dear for your sake. Rest assured that we will continue to work on your behalf. Power shall be entrusted to a government emanating from you and inspired by you. This can only be realized by the creation of a people's republic, which will uphold complete Iraqi unity, tie itself in bonds of fraternity with the Arab and Moslem states, . . .

From Hanna Batatu, *The Old Social Classes and the Revolutionary Movements of Iraq,* Princeton University Press, 1978.

Questions

1 How did Qassem's forces gain control of Baghdad?

2 Why was it necessary to broadcast Proclamation No. 1?

3 Was the Iraqi army united in its support for the coup?

4 What kind of people might support the overthrow of the government? Was there any danger that this support might get out of hand?

5 Who were the 'corrupt crew' and 'imperialism and its stooges' in Source B?

6 Does the evidence suggest that killing the royal family was or was not premeditated?

7 Read the last paragraph in Source A. What is the historian's opinion of the killing of Nuri and the Crown Prince? How far do you agree with his explanation for 'inhumaneness'?

25 Asad, Syria and the Middle East

Syria won independence when France gave up her mandate in 1945. In the next twenty-five years she was ruled by party coalitions or military governments. Between 1958 and 1961 she joined with Egypt in the United Arab Republic which was broken up by Syrian army officers. After that, the leading force in politics was the Ba'ath Party whose slogan was 'One Arab nation with an Eternal Mission'. In 1970, a socialist Ba'ath group led by a forty-year-old general, Hafez-al-Asad seized power. President Asad set out to rebuild the sort of position Syria had when she was one of the two great Arab provinces in the Ottoman Empire. This is illustrated by the Lebanese socialist, the Druze leader Kamal Joumblatt, in Source A. Asad's ambitions led to quarrels with Jordan and with Iraq. The Iraqis complained about the Syrian dam across the Euphrates river and Syrian support for Iran in the 'Gulf War'. Source B is taken from a fortnightly survey of events in the Arab world and Source C is by an Israeli political writer.

A A Lebanese view of Syria

The rulers of Damascus . . . do not want the Palestinians to forget . . . the days which preceded the divisions of the Middle East in 1919, when the Lebanese, Palestinians, Jordanians and Syrians were one people – the people of historic Syria in its natural boundaries . . .

From Kamal Joumblatt, *I speak for Lebanon*, Zed Books Ltd., 1982.

B Syria–Iraq dispute, 1975

The Minister of the Euphrates Dam, Subhi Kahhala, had given a press conference at which he cited statistics 'to refute the Iraqi fascist rightist rulers' lies about Syria which allege that Syria is withholding Euphrates river waters from the territory of fraternal Iraq', Damascus Radio reported on 7 May. Kahhala said that in 1974, 18,000 million cubic metres of water came from the Turkish borders, of which 9,000 million cubic metres had been released to Iraq . . . Kahhala accused Iraq of considering Syria 'purely as a waterway', and said that the Iraqi Government was not taking into account the bad rainfall season or the storing of water in the Khizan Dam in Turkey.

From *Arab Report and Record*, May 1–15, Issue 9, London, 1975.

C Asad's diplomacy, 1980

In 1980, after the alleged discovery of another Syrian plot in Baghdad, the Iraqi government expelled the Syrian ambassador, and Syria retaliated in the same fashion. With the eruption of the Iraqi–Iranian war . . . Syrian–Iraqi relations sank to their lowest ebb. This setback was soon followed by King Hussein's* decision finally to pull away from Asad and move towards a closer association with Iraq. Losing his last potential military ally against Israel, and an additional indirect link to the U.S., later in 1980 Asad moved several military divisions to the Jordanian border in an unsuccessful attempt to exert pressure on Hussein.

From Moshe Ma'oz, *Asad, the Sphinx of Damascus*, Weidenfeld and Nicolson, 1988.

* of Jordan

With the total collapse of his ambitious regional Arab strategy (except for close relations with the P.L.O.), bogged down in the Lebanese quagmire, exposed to a growing Israeli threat, and alienated again from the U.S. (following the Camp David accords), Asad finally agreed (or asked?) in October 1980 to sign a friendship and cooperation treaty with the Soviet Union.

D Syria and her neighbours

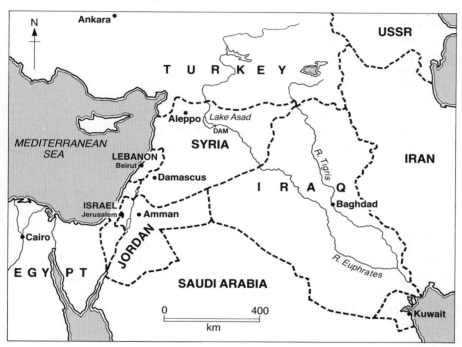

Questions

1 From the map and that in Unit 1, explain Joumblatt's view of Syrian ambitions.

2 Find the Euphrates Dam on the map. What clues do the map and Source B provide to possible causes of international disputes over water supplies?

3 Why do some governments call each other names like 'fascist rightist rulers'?

4 Use Source C to explain how Asad's 'ambitious regional Arab strategy' was collapsing in the cases of a) Iraq, b) Jordan, c) Lebanon, and d) Camp David.

5 What would be the difference if Asad had asked for a treaty with the USSR rather than agreeing to it?

6 Can you work out from the sources which side Syria supported in the Gulf War?

26 Qadhafi and Libya

Libya is mainly a desert state, one fifth the area of the USA. Nearly all Libyans live along the fertile Mediterranean coast or at inland oases. Until 1951, Libya was an Italian colony and was then ruled as an independent state by King Idris. On 1 September 1969 Idris was ousted by a Revolutionary Command Council led by 27-year-old Colonel Muammar Qadhafi, whose family were nomadic Berber people. The next year the USA and Britain handed over their military bases in Libya and in 1974 Qadhafi nationalised the oil industry. Libya's oil income rose steeply in the 1970s and was used to pay for military, industrial and agricultural programmes. In Source A an American researcher describes the changes he found at an inland oasis settlement, Augila, in 1977, eight years after a previous visit. He also describes the Libyan system of popular government. In 1978 Qadhafi resigned all his official posts and declared he would take the lead in a movement of Revolutionary Committees which would take Libya to the next step — Jamahiriya, or a state ruled by its people without a government. He described his role in Jamahiriya to a journalist in 1983 (Source B). However, by that time Libyan prosperity was declining with the slump in oil prices and there was discontent with Qadhafi's leadership.

A Augila, 1977

It was as if the quiet village I have previously depicted had become a bustling town overnight. Five new schools have been constructed, of which the secondary, girls and Koranic have been newly introduced to Augila. These are staffed by sixty or so Auragil*, Egyptians, Palestinians, Sudanese and Lebanese ... A modern hospital will be completed within a year's time. There are four full-time medical doctors now (Egyptian, Palestinian, Sudanese, Indian), in contrast to the once-a-week visiting doctor of eight years ago. Public housing has increased greatly; part of this houses professionals and workers from outside of Libya ...

* local people

In one fifteen minute period in the public square of the main village there were more cars parked than I had seen in the Oasis over a year's time. Small stores are bulging with goods. More money is available to everyone and there is much more to buy. Many homes have television sets and refrigerators. The new and increased incomes are deriving, not mainly from oil company labour (since the oil concessions in the regions have not expanded much), but from new employment opportunities in the public and private sectors. Improved garden production has occurred in relation to greater marketing possibilities. Vegetables can now be shipped to Benghazi in 7–10 hours in contrast to a day and a half. An agricultural cooperative gives farmers the chance to buy seeds, fertilizer, and equipment in bulk at reduced cost.

  ... Although I cannot speak for the rest of Libya, the new political structure formulated by Colonel Qadhafi and his associates have been highly effective in Augila ... (1) Popular councils determine needs based on consultation with the populace; (2) these are passed on to a regional council . . . which divide up the resources among the three communities; (3) for larger national questions, each local council sends three members to the collective council in Tripoli . . . The presence of these structures has had the effect of breaking down the old authority structure, based on the principles of the *mudir* and *qubail* (boss and tribes), . . . This system of self-government has been formulated in Colonel Qadhafi's *Green Book* . . . and is taught in the schools two hours per week. Almost all the people I talked to are very enthusiastic about the new system and the many positive changes it has brought about . . . Despite all the bad press on Colonel Qadhafi, his internal policy is working very successfully in Augila.

From John P. Mason, *Island of the Blest: Islam in a Libyan Oasis Community*, Ohio University, 1977.

B Jamahiriya

I lead the revolution. My mission is to instigate* the masses to practice authority. Authority, or power, is in the hands of the masses, through the people's congresses and the people's committees. I lead the movement of the Revolutionary Committees wherever there are revolutionary committees. Whether they are inside Libya or even abroad in the rest of the Arab world, I still preside over or lead this revolutionary movement of committees whose task is to realise the age of the era of the masses, in which the authority of the masses is achieved all over the world, so that we can do away with government . . .

* *persuade*

From J. Bearman, *Qadhafi's Libya*, Zed Books Ltd., 1986.

Questions

1 In what ways were people in Augila told about Qadhafi's ideas?

2 Why do you think there were so many foreign workers in Augila?

3 Describe the sort of issues you think would be decided by the three levels of government mentioned in Source A's third paragraph.

4 What does Source A suggest as a reason for introducing 'popular government' into Libya? How important do you think the change would be to a programme of modernisation?

5 Explain in your own words what Qadhafi meant by 'authority' and 'the masses' in Source B.

6 If the people already had their committees and congresses why do you think that Qadhafi believed they needed leadership from Revolutionary Committees?

7 Study Sources A and B carefully. Make lists of things that would give Qadhafi's government a) a 'good press', and b) a 'bad press' outside Libya.

27 Saudi Arabia

The desert monarchy of Saudi Arabia was carved out of the old Turkish Empire by the desert warrior prince, Abdul Aziz Ibn Saud, who became king in 1932. Arabia was little known to the outside world early in the twentieth century. Ibn Saud was a puritan Muslim who disliked motorcars and telephones. In the 1930s his government was short of money and he was forced to sell oil concessions to American oil companies.

The population benefited little at first from a growing oil industry. In the 1960s, King Faisal introduced a programme of reforms, which ranged from providing education for girls to building airports. Oil prices quadrupled between 1972 and 1974 and Saudi Arabia nationalised her oil industry. The extra revenues paid for industrial cities like Yanbu on the Red Sea and telecommunications systems and water de-salination plants. Thousands of highly-paid foreign technicians were flown in to help. In Source A, a British writer, Robert Lacey, describes how modernisation has affected Saudi city dwellers. The photograph was taken on the outskirts of the city of Dhahran, inland from the Arabian Gulf.

A Desert and city

It is six o'clock on a Friday evening, the end of the Kingdom's day of worship and rest. The roads are packed with cars. The traffic jams heading to town are made up principally of foreigners, the expatriate work force returning to their quarters, red-faced and sticky after their afternoon in the sun. The cars heading out of town contain the Saudis ... A mile or so out of town the traffic starts to thin. The road stretches straight ahead, a tarmac strip unrolled across the contours of the landscape. The houses get rarer – odd skeletons of breezeblock and prestressed concrete awaiting their marble cladding – and then there is just dusty red emptiness.

They go without warning, Mercedes, Cadillacs, Toyotas suddenly veering sideways across the crusted lip of the tarmac, to bump across the laterite* for several hundred yards . . . until each has found its own little patch of nothing.

A woven carpet is unrolled, some cushions are thrown down, little glass cups are set out on a silver tray, and from the vacuum flask is poured the tea – amber, clear and sweet. The men kick away their sandals and lift off their head-dresses. If no other cars are near, the women remove their veils. The children grab 7-Up from the cold box, or Pepsi. The women lean back against the hubcaps of the cars, digging sweets and lollies for the children from their bags. The men lean with their elbows on the cushions, gossiping gently, listening to the soccer results, or just gazing across the desert.

This is where they have come from. The desert is everything they hold dear – their religion, their code of honour, their ancestry, their black gold – and regularly the inhabitants of the Kingdom flee the

From Robert Lacey,
The Kingdom,
Hutchinson and Co.
(Publishers) Ltd., 1981.

* *desert soil*

modern pyramids their riches are creating to return to the bleak void that they find so consoling.

B A desert scene near Dhahran

Questions

1 What references to a traditional Arab way of life can be found in Source A?

2 How does the clothing worn by the man in the photograph suit him for his work?

3 From Sources A and B list examples of goods and technology that were imported into Saudi Arabia.

4 What differences between European and Arab ways of enjoying a day off does Robert Lacey point to?

5 Why should Saudis find the 'bleak void so consoling'? How might they explain the advantages and disadvantages of modernisation for their country?

6 How would you describe the differences between the modernisation programmes, and their effects on the lives of the people, in Saudi Arabia and Libya (Unit 26)?

28 Women in modern Islam

The Prophet Mohammed taught in the Koran that it was Allah's will that Muslim women should be treated fairly. They should be allowed to own property and have equal rights in marriage, though a man could take more than one wife. The Koran was open to interpretation on certain matters. Many Muslims felt that it forbade men and women to mix in public because that might lead to sinfulness. In the early twentieth century, Muslim women were usually treated unequally. In 1907, for instance, an Iranian law refused women and criminals the right to vote. Sixty years later, changes in their status were taking place. President Nasser's National Charter of 1962 established equal rights for women. In 1963 equal voting rights were granted to women in Iran. By the early 1980s a female's right to education was accepted by all Middle East countries. Of Saudi Arabia's 1.5 million student population, 40% were female. Yet many examples of traditional views still existed. Women in Saudi Arabia were forbidden to drive cars or travel without an accompanying male relative. Women themselves often accepted their traditional position, as did some of the prisoners in Source A. This is taken from the memoirs of an Egyptian woman doctor, Nawal el Sa'adawi, who was also a well known writer. She tells of her experience as a political prisoner in Egypt from September to November 1981. The photograph shows Shia women 'soldiers of Allah' parading in a Tehran street in 1982 during the Iran–Iraq war. Two years earlier the Shia leaders of Iran ruled that all women, including foreigners, had to wear a chador, *or veil, in public.*

A A political prisoner

Metal bunk beds. Bodies moving inside black cloaks. Heads wrapped in white or black; the higaab, which shields the head and neck, covering the wearer's hair completely. Faces concealed beneath niqaabs – all-enveloping face-veils with small holes through which I could perceive the steady gaze of human eyes . . . I could make out one of the faces under the yellow light, and I called out in delight. 'Safinaz!'

We hugged each other. She was a journalist and writer whom I hadn't seen for many years, and she had greatly changed. She hadn't been wearing a higaab then.

A pair of eyes were gazing at me through two holes in a black niqaab. 'Who is our new colleague?'

'Dr. Nawal el Sa'adawi,' answered Safinaz. 'Author of dangerous books full of heresy.'

I saw a body moving on an upper bunk; she rose suddenly from her sleep and called out 'Greetings, Nawal.'

It was Dr. Amina Rashid, a professor at Cairo University. Having met her a number of times in gatherings at my house and in the homes of friends, we had become friends. Happy to see Amina, I embraced her as Safinaz asked, 'Have you read the books Nawal has published?'

'Of course I've read them,' Amina replied, 'and my women students at the University have, too. They asked me to invite Nawal to the

From Nawal el Sa'adawi, *Memoirs from the Women's Prison*, The Women's Press, 1986.

College so they could talk with her. These are important books which many people admire and like.'

'They're the books of an unbeliever and an atheist,' Safinaz responded.

'Have you read them?' Amina wanted to know.

'I read only the book of God.'

'How can you judge books which you haven't read?'

A moment of silence passed. Some of the young women in niqaabs began probing me with questions about these books. Two eyeholes approached me and I heard a voice asking 'Do you pray? Do you fast during Ramadan? Isn't a woman's face a blemish upon her, a shameful private part to be covered?'

'The shameful blemishes are oppression, falsehood, and the eradication of the human mind, whether a woman's or a man's,' I said. . . .

The eyes inside the holes widened and took on a shine.

B Shia women soldiers

Each rifle has a flower in its muzzle

Questions

1 What evidence do the sources provide of attempts to enforce strict Muslim rules on women's dress?

2 In which ways had Safinaz changed in dress and beliefs since Nawal had last met her (Source A)?

3 How does one of the women in the prison cell explain her dress?

4 What arguments and evidence might a strict Muslim use to suggest that Nawal was an 'unbeliever'?

5 What effect might her books have had on women students?

6 Put in your own words how Nawal might have answered criticism of her attitudes.

Part 5

Israel and her neighbours, 1967–82

29 Israel: from agriculture to industry

In 1949, Israel was chiefly an agricultural country but less than 10 per cent of its land was cultivated. Some of the farming was done collectively by groups of people living together in kibbutzim. Source A is from an information sheet about Kibbutz Yiron, a mile from the border with Lebanon. By the early 1980s there were 250 kibbutzim holding about 3½ per cent of Israel's population. Source B, from a booklet published by the Kibbutz Movement, shows how kibbutzim had changed their earlier policy of keeping to pioneer farming. Source C illustrates the growing importance of industry to Israel's overseas earnings. The diagrams are based on figures taken from the London Economist. *Despite the changes Israel still had a trade deficit of $4 billion in 1985. Since 1949 her annual trade gap has been bridged mostly by loans from the United States government and cash donations from American Jews.*

A   Kibbutz Yiron

Yiron was founded by graduates of an urban Israeli youth movement who received agricultural training at veteran kibbutzim. During the Israeli War of Independence in 1948, they enlisted and fought together in the same region where they later built their home.

From the Centre for Kibbutz Studies, Efal Seminar, 1983.

In 1949 the group settled at the present-day site of the kibbutz which was chosen in order to strengthen the sparse Jewish population in the area. Over the course of time they were joined by Jewish immigrants from Egypt and by additional graduates of urban Israeli youth movements. In 1953, as a result of an ideological–political split in the kibbutz movement, part of the membership left Yiron.

Population: approximately 400, including 140 members and 165 children . . .

Agriculture: Yiron farms 1250 acres of land. Major agricultural branches include cotton, orchards, avocados, poultry and a dairy barn.

Industry: the kibbutz's 'Paskal' factory manufactures plastic zippers.

B   Farm versus factory

Once, we argued a lot about factories and the nature of our communities. Some kibbutzim wanted to maintain small, intimate communities based on farming the land . . . For these kibbutzim, the

From Joel Magid, *Kibbutz: the way we live*, Federation of the Kibbutz Movements, 1980.

factory was to be shunned, to be banned from the kibbutz because of its dehumanizing effect on workers. Other kibbutzim believed that the socialist kibbutz had a national duty to grow large and to absorb as many people as possible in a mixed economy of farming, handicrafts and industry.

Reality, however, has its way of transforming . . . ideology. A limited amount of water and arable land in our dry country, the rapid absorption of agricultural technology and the growth in population of the kibbutz made us turn to factories in order to guarantee our economic viability in the face of fickle rain gods and in order to provide members with workplaces where they could contribute to the society. So we built factories; now almost every kibbutz has a factory and some of the larger kibbutzim even have two or three different industrial enterprises.

C Israel's exports, 1958–85

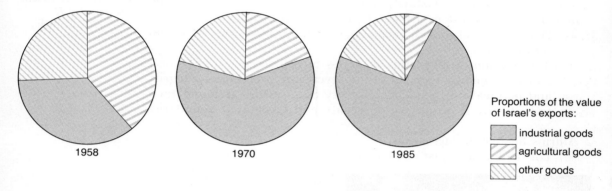

1958   1970   1985

Proportions of the value
of Israel's exports:

industrial goods
agricultural goods
other goods

Questions

1 Use the first part of Sources A and B to describe the ideals of the pioneers who set up the early kibbutzim.

2 What reason is given for some members leaving Kibbutz Yiron in 1953? How might Source B help to explain their departure?

3 Explain what 'ideology' means in the second paragraph of Source B. Make a list of the 'realities' which forced kibbutzim to change.

4 What step was taken in Kibbutz Yiron to meet the need for the 'economic viability' referred to in Source B?

5 What does Source C tell you about the developments in Israel's economy between 1958 and 1985? What effect do you think this had on kibbutzim?

6 Write down arguments for and against changing kibbutzim from being 'communities based on farming the land' to communities practising 'a mixed economy'.

30 Six Day War, 1967

The Six Day War began on 5 June 1967 when the Israel Defence Force (IDF) struck suddenly at the country's three most powerful Arab neighbours. By 10 June the IDF controlled all Palestine up to the Jordan and had dramatically weakened Egypt by reaching the Suez Canal, and Syria by taking the Golan Heights. The self-confident mood of Israel's troops can be judged from the IDF greetings card for the Jewish New Year in September 1967. Hundreds of thousands of Palestinians were refugees or living in the Occupied Territories. Britain put Resolution 242 to the Security Council of the UN in November. Israel accepted it and so did Egypt and Jordan, but not Syria.

A Security Council Resolution 242

1 Affirms that the fulfilment of Charter principles requires the establishment of a just and lasting peace in the Middle East which should include the application of both the following principles:

  (i) Withdrawal of Israeli armed forces from territories of recent conflict;

  (ii) Termination of all claims or states of belligerency and respect for and acknowledgement of the sovereignty, territorial integrity and political independence of every State in the area and their right to live in peace within secure and recognised boundaries . . .

2 Affirms further the necessity . . .

  (b) For achieving a just settlement of the refugee problem . . .

From The Origins and Evolution of the Palestine Problem, Part II: 1947–1977, United Nations, 1979.

B   New Year greetings

The words in Hebrew at the top mean 'Armed Forces of Israel'

C

The end of the war

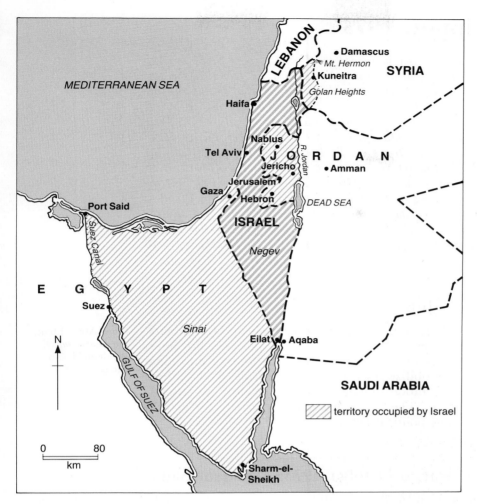

Questions

1 What does Resolution 242 ask a) Israel, and b) Egypt, Jordan, Syria and Iraq to do?

2 Israel accepted the Resolution. Suggest why she believed she could stay in the Occupied Territories.

3 What might the refugees have thought about the Resolution?

4 What does the greetings card tell you about a) the morale of the IDF in late 1967, and b) a war gain which would especially please many Israelis?

5 Use the map to explain the importance to Israel of each territory it occupied.

6 With the help of the map suggest the most important consequence of the war for each of: the Palestinians, Jordan, Egypt, and Syria.

31 Yom Kippur, 1973

In January 1970 President Nasser persuaded the USSR to send SAM missiles and military advisers to Egypt. Shortly after, Nasser died. In July 1972 the new President, Anwar Sadat, expelled the Soviet advisers in an effort to win support from the USA, but the missile build-up went on. Source A shows how an Israeli general, Yitzhak Rabin, rated the threat for a newspaper in July 1973. Three months later the Arab states launched a joint attack on 6 October, the eve of the Jewish festival of Yom Kippur. In Source B, President Sadat recalls that day in an interview with a British reporter. Source C is from a radio broadcast on 6 October by the Israeli prime minister, Mrs Golda Meir. By mid-October the Arab forces appeared to be doing well and this is reflected in a speech by President Asad of Syria (Source D) and the cartoon in an Egyptian newspaper. By the cease-fire on 26 October the Israelis had forced the Syrians off the Golan heights and crossed the Suez Canal to within 100 km of Cairo. Yet, the IDF had suffered severe losses.

A Yitzhak Rabin, 13 July 1973

There is no need to mobilize our forces whenever we hear Arab threats, or when the enemy concentrates his forces along the ceasefire lines. Before the Six-Day War, any movement of Egyptian forces into Sinai would compel Israel to mobilize reserves on a large scale. Today, there is no need for such mobilization so long as Israel's defence line extends along the Suez Canal ... The Arabs have little capacity for coordinating their military and political action.

From Abba Eban, *An Autobiography*, Weidenfeld and Nicolson, 1977.

B The outbreak of war, 6 October 1973: President Sadat

I was under terrific tension, frozen. We didn't know what the Israelis had in store. What new weapons did they have? But after three hours it was clear that the Israelis had not mobilized and had been totally surprised. Our troops made their crossing over the steep canal sides ...

From *Sunday Times* 'Insight' team, *Yom Kippur War*, André Deutsch, 1975.

C Mrs Golda Meir, 6 October 1973

Citizens of Israel, at around 1400 today the armies of Egypt and Syria launched an offensive against Israel ... The IDF* is fighting back and repulsing the attack. The enemy has suffered serious losses ... They hoped to surprise the citizens of Israel on the Day of Atonement* while many were praying at the synagogues ... But we were not surprised ... A few days ago the Israeli intelligence service learned that the armies of Egypt and Syria were deployed for a coordinated attack ... Our forces were deployed as necessary to meet the danger. We have no doubt about our victory.

From *Sunday Times* 'Insight' team, *Yom Kippur War*, André Deutsch, 1975.

* Israeli Defence Force
* Festival of Yom Kippur. The date also lies within the Muslim Festival of Ramadan

D President Hafez-al-Asad of Syria, 15 October 1973

Our heroes have transformed Israel's aggression, since 6 October, to a retreat of the enemy forces. As I told you on that day our forces rushed to repulse the aggression, forcing the occupation forces to withdraw before them. They continued their advance and expelled the enemy forces from Mount Hermon, Kuneitra ... and other villages and positions in the Golan ...

From W. Laqueur and B. Rubin (eds.), *The Israel–Arab Reader* (4th Edition), Facts on File Publications, 1985.

E  Egyptian view, 12 October 1973

This cartoon was titled 'Scare-crow'. On the central pillar is written 'The Army that cannot be beaten'. The dates 1948, 1956 and 1967 are on the helmet and the arms

Questions

1 What evidence is there in Sources A, B and D that Israel had not withdrawn from lands occupied in 1967?

2 Does Source A give any hints that some Israelis were concerned about Arab military plans?

3 Which two kinds of reason has Rabin for saying there was no threat?

4 Do Sources B and C suggest that attacking on 6 October gave the Arabs an advantage?

5 What did Mrs Meir hope to achieve by making her broadcast?

6 In Source D what does Asad mean by 'occupation forces'?

7 Which army is shown in the cartoon? What do the three dates refer to?

8 How might Syrians and Egyptians reading Asad's speech and seeing the cartoon have felt about the war?

32 Camp David, 1978

After his election in 1976, President Jimmy Carter continued the efforts of the United States to gain the respect of both sides in the Arab–Israeli dispute. In March 1977, Carter said that a homeland should be found for the Palestinian people. On 1 October 1977, the United States and Soviet Russia together declared their wish for a 'just and lasting settlement of the Arab–Israeli conflict'. On 9 November 1977, President Sadat of Egypt announced that he was prepared to visit Israel. Eleven days later he addressed Israel's Knesset, or Parliament, on the need to solve the problems that separated Israel from its Arab opponents. He was condemned by the Arab world for his visit. In August 1978, President Carter invited Sadat and the Israeli Prime Minister, Menachem Begin, to talks at Camp David, the President's official country home.

A key issue for Begin was whether the Knesset would vote to give up the Israeli bases and settlements in Sinai. Source A, from President Carter's memoirs, describes the moment when Begin agreed to try to persuade the Knesset. Source B, from the memoirs of Israel's foreign minister, described the Knesset debate when the opposition leader criticised the Sinai arrangements but still said he would vote for them. Egyptian opponents of Sadat objected to Egypt signing a peace treaty without the other Arab states and without settling the question of Arab refugees in Gaza and the West Bank. The Egyptian foreign minister resigned over this issue during the Camp David talks and Source C is his account of the protest he made to Sadat.

A Carter and Begin, 16 September 1978.

Cy* and I ate some crackers and cheese as I listed the benefits of the proposed agreements to Israel. Immediately Begin began talking about the blessed settlements, but I insisted that we go through both documents in an orderly fashion, . . .

I thought the discussion would never end. It was obviously very painful for Prime Minister Begin, who was shouting words like 'ultimatum', 'excessive demands' and 'political suicide'. However, he finally promised to submit to the Knesset within two weeks the question: 'If agreement is reached on all other Sinai issues, will the settlers be withdrawn?'

I believed this concession would be enough for Sadat. Breakthrough!

* Cyrus Vance, US Secretary of State

From Jimmy Carter, *Keeping Faith*, Collins, 1982.

B The Knesset debate

. . . the Leader of the Opposition, Shimon Peres . . . began, unexpectedly, by congratulating the Prime Minister and the Government on 'the difficult, awesome, but vital decision they had taken to secure peace at a price which had been thought impossible for this Government' . . . Peres, as befitted an Opposition leader, moved from praise to sharp criticism both of the agreement and the way the negotiations were conducted. He charged us with paying the price of mistakes

From Moshe Dayan, *Breakthrough*, Weidenfeld and Nicolson, 1981.

which could have been avoided . . . We had given up a defensible border and conceded Sinai airfields, and he thought we could have done better on both these points . . . The evacuation of our Sinai settlements, too, could have been avoided . . .

. . . the Leader of the Opposition had perforce to explain why, then, he was supporting the Government's resolution. To do so, he extolled* *praised* Sadat's initiative, and indicated that voting against the Government would be interpreted as spurning the outstretched Egyptian hand and questioning the value of the Camp David Conference. This would gravely damage the chances of peace, and our relations with the United States.

C Egyptian opposition

I have read the project presented to you yesterday by President Carter on the framework for peace, and have concluded that it is extremely unlikely to result in the comprehensive peace at which you are aiming, whose broad lines you . . . clearly defined in your speech to the Knesset when you visited Jerusalem. The American project leads to a separate peace between Egypt and Israel which would be completely independent of what might happen in the West Bank and Gaza . . . there will be a peace treaty between Egypt and Israel while the West Bank and Gaza remain in the possession and under the domination of Israel. The latter will then proceed to implement its schemes for the final annexation of those territories.

With regard to this . . . we have no mandate from the representatives of the Palestinian people . . . or from the Arab states whom, one and all, share the responsibility for solving the Palestinian problem . . .

I therefore implore . . . you to refuse to sign such a ruinous agreement.

From Mohammed Ibrahim Kamel, *The Camp David Accords*, K.P.I. Ltd., 1986.

Questions

1 Use Sources A and B, and the map on Page 61, to explain why Begin was concerned about the Sinai issue.

2 What was the 'breakthrough', according to President Carter in Source A?

3 In your own words explain why Shimon Peres a) criticised the deal, and b) agreed to support it.

4 What are the three key points made by the foreign minister against a treaty in Source C?

5 Which pieces of evidence in the extracts most help to explain Israel's wish for a peace agreement with Egypt?

6 From these sources which of Sadat or Begin do you think had most to lose from signing the treaty between Israel and Egypt in March 1979?

33 Israel invades the Lebanon, 1982

On 3 June 1982, Israel's ambassador to London was wounded by a Palestinian group who were rivals of the PLO. Israel's prime minister, Menachem Begin, blamed the PLO and used the attack as the excuse for invading Lebanon, where the PLO had its main bases. Source A is from the government's statement on 6 June. Within forty-eight hours the Israeli Defence Force (IDF) had occupied southern Lebanon and the defence minister, Ariel Sharon, ordered them to go on to destroy Syrian missile bases further north, around the Damascus–Beirut road. Source B is an Israeli journalist's record of an IDF officer's opinion of this order. PLO and Syrian forces were soon trapped in Beirut and forced to leave the country. Israeli forces now controlled West Beirut. On 17 and 18 September they stood by while extremist Christian Lebanese militia massacred several hundred Palestinian men, women and children in the refugee camps of Sabra and Chatilla. Many people inside and outside Israel held her government responsible. The cartoon is from the British Guardian *and Source C is from a speech by the leader of the Israeli opposition at a meeting attended by 400,000 people in Tel Aviv.*

A   Israel announces invasion, 6 June 1982

The Cabinet took the following decision:
1 To instruct the IDF to place all the civilian population of the Galilee beyond the range of the terrorist fire from Lebanon where they, their bases and their headquarters are concentrated.
2 The name of the operation is Peace for Galilee.
3 During the operation, the Syrian army will not be attacked unless it attacks our forces.
4 Israel continues to aspire to the signing of a peace treaty with independent Lebanon, its territorial integrity preserved.

From Conor Cruise O'Brien, *The Siege*, Weidenfeld and Nicolson, 1986.

B   An Israeli army commander

What does the Beirut–Damascus highway have to do with the peace of the Galilee? . . . Why do we find ourselves on the attack and hear the IDF spokesman announce that it was the Syrians who opened fire? What have we got against the Syrians? I want you to know that the consensus* has been shattered – around here, at least – and with alarming signs of a breakdown in credibility.

From Ze'ev Schiff and Eliud Ya'ari, *Israel's Lebanon War*, George Allen and Unwin, 1985.

general agreement

C   Shimon Peres, Israeli Labour Party leader

People from all communities throughout the country have come here to express their shock at the terrible massacre and to say 'This government does not represent us.' This war's declared objective, peace for Galilee, had been obtained, but the war continues and nobody knows for what reason. Begin and Sharon, you knew first about the massacre. Why did you not appoint an investigation at once?

From *Jerusalem Post*, 26 September 1982.

D 'We did not know what was going on . . .'

The figure in front of the tank represents Menachem Begin and the figure in the turret, Ariel Sharon

From the *Guardian*, 20 September 1982.

Questions

1 What was the government suggesting by calling the invasion operation 'Peace for Galilee'?

2 How far into Lebanon were Israeli forces supposed to go, according to Source A?

3 How does Source B show that the Israeli cabinet quickly changed its mind?

4 What did the Israeli officer mean when he referred to a 'breakdown in credibility'? How is his view supported by Shimon Peres in Source C?

5 Why is the tank in the cartoon labelled 'Happy New Year'?

6 Explain the cartoonist's view of Begin's and Sharon's part in the massacres.

7 Can you identify the two main criticisms that Peres is making in Source C?

Part 6

The Palestinians

34 Palestine Liberation Organisation

In 1964 Egypt encouraged the leaders of Palestinian refugees to form the Palestine Liberation Organisation under her guidance. After Egypt and other Arab countries were defeated by Israel in 1967, the PLO decided that it had to carry out its own struggle. The claim that Palestine was their country was set out in the 1968 National Charter (Source A). In 1969 it became a much stronger organisation when it was joined by the guerrilla group, Al-Fatah, whose leader Yasser Arafat became chairman of the PLO. In 1974 the United Nations voted to recognise the PLO as the representatives of the Palestinian people and Yasser Arafat was invited to address the General Assembly – where the Israeli Ambassador stated his country's refusal to accept PLO claims (Source B and C). The PLO's main support has always come from the refugee camps, first mostly in Jordan and then in Lebanon. Source D is a report by United Nations officials after complaints that PLO guerrillas were using a United Nations Relief and Works Agency (UNRWA) educational centre in Lebanon as a base.

A Palestinian National Charter, 1968

1 Palestine is the homeland of the Arab Palestinian people . . .
2 Palestine, with the boundaries it had during the British Mandate, is an indivisible territorial unit . . .
5 The Palestinians are those Arab nationals who, until 1947, normally resided in Palestine regardless of whether they were evicted from it or have stayed there. Anyone born, after that date, of a Palestinian father – whether inside Palestine or outside it – is also a Palestinian.
6 The Jews who had normally resided in Palestine until the beginning of the Zionist invasion will be considered Palestinians.
7 . . . All means of information and education must be adapted in order to acquaint the Palestinian with his country . . . He must be prepared for the armed struggle and ready to sacrifice his wealth and his life in order to win back his homeland and bring about its liberation . . .

From W. Laqueur and B. Rubin (eds.), *The Israel–Arab Reader* (4th Edition), Facts on File Publications, 1985.

B Arafat addresses the UN, 13 November 1974

. . . as Chairman of the Palestine Liberation Organization and leader of the Palestinian revolution . . . I appeal to you to enable our people to establish national independent sovereignty over its own land.

Today I have come bearing an olive branch and a freedom-fighter's

From W. Laqueur and B. Rubin (eds.), *The Israel–Arab Reader* (4th Edition), Facts on File Publications, 1985.

gun. Do not let the olive branch fall from my hand. I repeat: do not let the olive branch fall from my hand.

C The Israeli ambassador, 13 November 1974

Israel will not permit the establishment of P.L.O. authority in any part of Palestine. The P.L.O. will not be forced on the Palestinian Arabs. It will not be tolerated by the Jews of Israel.

From T. G. Fraser (ed.), *The Middle East 1914–1979*, Edward Arnold, 1980.

D The PLO in southern Lebanon

UNRWA has completed an internal investigation into the protest by the Government of Israel, alleging misuse for military purposes of the Agency's Siblin Training Centre near Sidon, Lebanon. The Centre provides vocational and teacher training to young Palestine refugees.

From *UNRWA Press Release*, HQ/31/82, 22 October 1982.

The investigation found evidence of misuse of the Centre before June 1982, beginning probably at the end of 1979 or early in 1980. The Centre's principal has been suspended . . .

The investigation has revealed that from 6 to 15 PLO military personnel had been permitted to occupy rooms adjacent to the Centre's dormitories and had the use of three rooms near the Centre's clinic. They evidently also had the exclusive use of the basement of the clinic in which some radio equipment had been installed and files, food, arms, ammunition and other equipment stored. The Centre's premises had also been used to provide military training to the students, consisting of lectures and basic weapons training, although no firing practice took place on the Centre's grounds.

Questions

1 Explain what the Charter meant by 'an indivisible territorial unit'. How did this statement challenge Israel?

2 According to the Charter, who was a Palestinian?

3 In which two main ways were Palestinians called on to win back their homeland?

4 What evidence is there of one of these ways in Sources B and D?

5 How is Source B evidence that the PLO was influential in 1974?

6 What does Source C tell you about the Israeli view of the PLO's claims?

7 Do you think the evidence supports the UN's view that the training centre was being misused?

8 Is it surprising that camps and refugee training centres were often centres for PLO activity? Why should Israel complain about this?

35 Palestinian refugees

About 700,000 Palestinians took refuge in neighbouring Arab states and the Gaza strip during the war of 1948–1949. Camps such as the one in the photograph of Nahr el Bared in north Lebanon in 1949 were set up by the United Nations Relief and Works Agency (UNRWA). General Burns, a Canadian former commander of the UN peace-keeping force, describes the Gaza camps in the mid 1950s (Source B). During the Six Day War, nearly half a million more Palestinians fled from the West Bank and Gaza. In Source C, a Palestinian Arab writer, Ahmed Baha Ed-Dine, talks about other Palestinians in the 1960s. In 1987, over 2.2 million Palestinians were registered as refugees in Jordan, Syria, Lebanon and the Israeli-occupied territories.

A   A refugee camp, 1949

B   Refugees in Gaza, mid-1950s

The 210,000 refugees are fed by the United Nations Relief and Works Agency. The standard ration provides 1600 calories a day, mostly carbohydrates. By Western standards 1600 calories is a reducing diet ...

They live in little huts of mud and concrete blocks, corrugated iron roofs, regimented row after row. Fairly adequate medical service is provided, probably better than they enjoyed before they were expelled

From E. L. M. Burns, *Between Arab and Israeli*, George Harrap and Co., 1962.

from their native villages. It is especially good in the maternity and child-care clinics, with the result that the infant death rate is low. Children swarm everywhere. There are primary schools for nearly all of them – little girls in cotton dresses with fine black and white stripes, little boys in khaki shirts and shorts. There are secondary schools for a good proportion of the adolescents; and a great number of youths can always be seen, around examination times, strolling along the roads memorizing their lessons: where else could they concentrate to study? And what will all these youths and girls do when they have finished their secondary school training? There is no employment for them in the Strip, and very few can leave it to work elsewhere . . . One does not see people starving or dying of disease in the streets; nevertheless the Gaza Strip resembles a vast concentration camp, shut off by the sea, the border between Palestine and the Sinai near Rafah, which the Egyptians will not permit them to cross, and the Armistice Demarcation Line which they cross in peril of being shot by Israelis or imprisoned by the Egyptians. They can look to the east and see wide fields, once Arab land, cultivated extensively by a few Israelis, with a chain of *kibbutzim* guarding the heights or the areas beyond.

C The outlook for Palestinians, 1960s

The Palestinian faced the following dilemma: either to become a powerless refugee living in tents, or to become an ex-Palestinian emigrant in some other part of the world – Canada, Latin America or one of the Arab countries from Algeria to the West to Kuwait in the East.

Who emigrated? The most capable, competent and gifted of Palestine's sons. Those who had succeeded in their careers as businessmen, engineers, doctors, economists and journalists.

From W. Laqueur and B. Rubin (eds.), *The Israel–Arab Reader* (4th Edition), Facts on File Publications, 1985.

Questions

1 What facts about living conditions can be gained from the photograph?

2 In which ways does Source B suggest that conditions improved later?

3 Suggest why the Palestinians took education so seriously when they had little chance of having careers?

4 Do you think General Burns was justified in calling the Gaza Strip a 'vast concentration camp'?

5 Why is a Palestinian in the 1960s described as 'powerless' (Source C)? Is there evidence in Unit 34 to suggest that refugees had become more powerful later?

6 What responsibilities do members of the United Nations have for the care and protection of Palestinian refugees?

36 West Bank

In 1949 the 'West Bank' was separated from the rest of Palestine. In April 1950 King Abdullah took it into his kingdom of Jordan, along with east Jerusalem. As a result of the Six Day War in 1967, east Jerusalem became part of Israel and the West Bank (along with the Gaza strip) an Occupied Territory. In 1988 Jordan said she no longer claimed the West Bank as part of her territory.

Israeli governments encouraged Jewish settlements. By 1987 there were 118 with fifty-two per cent of the land under Israeli state control. The Arab population was then about one million while Jewish settlers numbered rather more than 70,000. The map shows the distribution of many of the settlements and Source A is a settler's account in an Israeli newspaper in 1978 of how some came by their land. Sources B and C concern employment. In B, a Christian Arab businessman talks about the effects of occupation on a local industry in Bethlehem. Source C is from the 1986 report of an independent team of researchers which was led by a Jewish former deputy mayor of Jerusalem.

A Jewish settlement

Here in the Jordan valley we are cultivating a thousand dunam* of rich, fertile farmland. This is – let's be honest about it – Arab land ... the land of 'absentees', people from Nablus and Tubas who fled to Jordan during the six-day war. These people cannot come back to Judaea and Samaria because the troops at the bridges have lists of names. The people in charge at the bridges are strict, and if you are an absentee landowner they just won't let you in ... Some of the absentees' land wasn't suitable for settlement, either it was too stony or too remote ... so we exchanged it for the land of Arabs still living here. Do you think they wanted to move out? We put, as you might say, pressure on them – we, the government, the military administration, the army.

* The Turkish word for ¼ acre of land

From Abdallah Frangi, *The P.L.O. and Palestine*, Zed Books Ltd., 1983.

B Arab industry

During the Jordanian regime the mother-of-pearl business reached its peak. Lots of tourists were coming; people learned how to develop it, and they did a good job. After the occupation of our country, the Israelis also did their best to help ... On the other hand, cost of living has almost doubled on the West Bank, even though we earn more money, the money doesn't buy as much as it should or as before the war. Now we are suffering from shortage of labour, because we are about five miles distant from Jerusalem ...

It takes, for example, three years to train a craftsman to do mother-of-pearl carving. Then for any simple reason this craftsman will just leave and go to work in Jerusalem ... they drain skilled labour from this area into their own district ... and unless we export our handicrafts abroad, a lot of our people do not find work.

From F. H. Epp, *The Palestinians: portrait of a people in conflict*, McClelland and Stewart, 1976.

C Employment report

An estimated 90,000 workers from the West Bank and Gaza cross the Green Line* daily to work in Israel. Less than half of this number are workers legally registered through the government Employment Service. Half of the labourers from the territories work in construction (48.3%), 19.5% are in services including low-status, low-paying employment as cleaners, gardeners and dishwashers. Eighteen per cent are in industry and 14.2% are in agriculture.

boundary between Israel and the Occupied Territories
From Meron Benvenisti, *1986 Report*, West Bank Data Base Project, Jerusalem, 1986.

D The West Bank

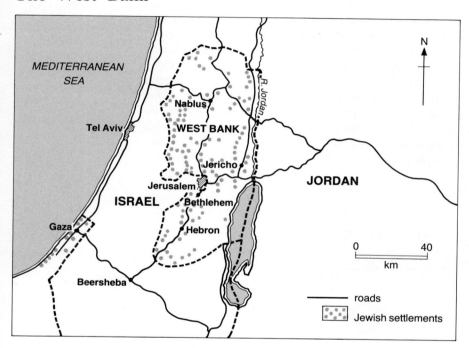

Questions

1 What does the map tell you about Jewish settlement after 1967? Suggest three reasons why Israeli governments encouraged it.

2 Why is the West Bank referred to as 'Judaea and Samaria' in Source A?

3 How reliable is Source A likely to be about Israeli government actions?

4 In which different ways was Bethlehem business affected by the Israeli occupation?

5 In which ways do B and C agree about the employment situation in the West Bank?

6 Use the sources to write a dialogue between a supporter and an opponent of Israel's occupation of the West Bank after 1967.

37 Jerusalem

For centuries, Jewish, Christian and Muslim pilgrims have prayed in the synagogues, churches and mosques of Jerusalem, which is holy to them all. It had been the capital of the Jewish kingdoms of Israel and Judah around 1000 BC when the first temple was built on Temple Mount. Jerusalem then fell to the Roman emperors who became Christian in the fourth century AD. That led to the building of Christian shrines such as the Church of the Holy Sepulchre which contains the supposed tomb of Christ. In the seventh century, Jerusalem was visited by the prophet Mohammed and was later conquered by Muslims. They built their holy places, the Dome of the Rock and the Al-Aqsa Mosque, on the Temple Mount. All that remained for Jews was part of the wall supporting one side of the Mount. This became the Wailing Wall where Jews prayed for their lost city and temple.

Source A is a postage stamp issued in 1938 by Palestinian Arab guerrillas. It shows the Al-Aqsa Mosque and the Holy Sepulchre, but no Jewish holy place. (Most Palestinian Arabs are Muslim, but some are Christian.) Source B gives King Abdullah's orders to his Arab Legion when war broke out in 1948. After the war, Jerusalem was divided between Israel and Jordan (see Map C) but the Israelis declared it was their capital. In the 1967 war east Jerusalem was taken by the Israelis. Israel has respected the holy Muslim places on the Temple Mount but militant Jews view it as theirs, as the 1987 newspaper report (D) shows.

A An Arab guerrilla stamp, 1938

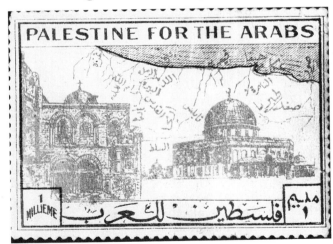

PALESTINE FOR THE ARABS

B King Abdullah's orders

The importance of Jerusalem in the eyes of the Arabs and the Muslims and the Arab Christians is well known. Any disaster suffered by the people of the city at the hands of the Jews – whether they were killed or driven from their homes – would have the most far-reaching results for us . . . I accordingly order that everything we hold today must be preserved – the Old City and the road to Jericho*.

From J. B. Glubb, *A Soldier with the Arabs*, Hodder and Stoughton, 1957.

* *an ancient town near to the River Jordan*

C Jerusalem, 1948–67

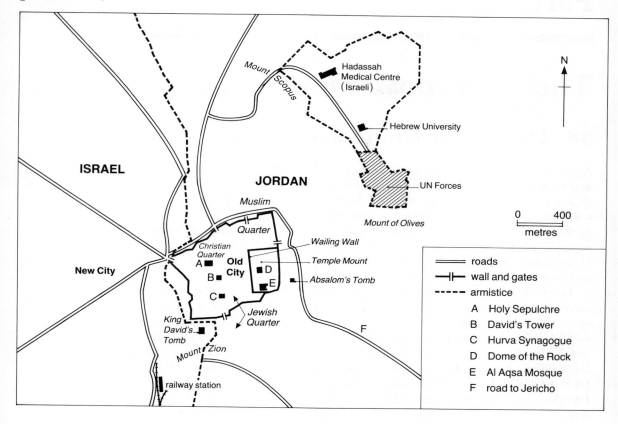

D 'Panic at Wailing Wall'

Jerusalem: thousands of Jewish worshippers and tourists fled Jerusalem's Wailing Wall in panic yesterday, as Israeli police used tear gas
and fired in the air to disperse Muslim protesters. About 2000 Palestinians chanting 'God is great' threw stones and bottles at 200 police
to protest against an attempt by militant Jews to enter the Temple
Mount, the site of the Al-Aqsa and Dome of the Rock mosques, . . .

From the *Guardian*,
London, 12 October
1987.

Questions

1 List the religious places on
the map. What do Sources A,
C and D tell you of the
significance of Jerusalem?

2 How does Source A explain
the Arab view about
Jerusalem as a holy city?

3 What were Abdullah's
instructions in May 1948?

4 What evidence from the map
shows that these were carried
out?

5 How does Source D illustrate
how past events may affect
behaviour today?

Part 7

The Superpowers

38 The Soviet Union and Egypt

Egypt's Colonel Nasser moved closer to the USSR when he agreed a Soviet arms deal with communist Czechoslovakia in 1955. The USA and Britain then withdrew their promise of loans for the Nile Dam. By 1957, half of Egypt's foreign trade was with Soviet bloc countries. In December 1959, the Soviet Union agreed to finance the Nile Dam, providing that the work was undertaken by Soviet engineers using Soviet equipment. Nasser accepted this, but was careful not to let his country become a Soviet satellite. This is clear in Source A, from a British journalist's history of the first phase of the dam project.

The Soviet Union gave extensive military aid to Egypt, following Israel's occupation of Egyptian Sinai in the Six Day War of 1967. By 1971, Egypt had received 450 MiG fighters, 1350 tanks and a number of SAM missiles. Approximately 19,500 Soviet advisers were stationed there. Nasser's successor, President Sadat, signed a treaty of friendship with the USSR in May 1971, but he accused his political opponents in Egypt of being Soviet agents and put many in prison. On 8 July 1972, Sadat told the Soviet Union to withdraw its advisers. The Soviet President, Leonid Brezhnev, asked for an explanation. Source B is an extract from Sadat's letter of reply in October 1972.

A Soviet aid

If Khruschev had assumed that Soviet aid for the High Dam would turn the U.A.R.* into an obedient satellite he was by this time disillusioned to the point of exasperation by the positiveness of President Nasser's neutrality . . . Russia particularly opposed his collaboration with Tito* in fostering a 'bloc' of neutral states which seemed likely to impede the extension of Soviet influence in the small and emerging nations. Above all, the indigenous* communist parties were having a rough time as the Arab revolution spread in the Middle East . . . President Nasser kept his communists securely locked up . . . The Soviet press castigated* the U.A.R. for its anti-communist policy and Mohammed Hassamein Heikal, editor of Al-Ahram and confidant of President Nasser, replied firmly that Soviet Russia was one thing, communism another, and Russia should keep its nose out of the internal affairs of friendly states . . .

The Egyptians suspected that the Russians were deliberately delaying the supply of equipment and they themselves were excessively

From Tom Little, *High Dam at Aswan*, Methuen and Co. Ltd., 1965.
* *United Arab Republic of Egypt and Syria*

* *President of Yugoslavia*

* *local*

* *criticized*

slow in implementing a training programme agreed in the spring of 1961, reportedly because President Nasser was reluctant to have communists running loose at Aswan in the guise of instructors.

B President Sadat to President Brezhnev, October 1972

Your letter of July 8 totally ignores our earlier agreement on the measures required to render us capable of making a military move, following the American elections, should this become necessary. America is now in the process of equipping Israel with an entirely new airforce. The attitude reflected in your latest letter shows that for five years a partial arms embargo had been imposed on us, and that this covers the deterrent arms which I wrote to you about and which you have completely ignored. These are the considerations which led to my decision to terminate the experts' mission . . .

i The Navy. For four years the commander of the navy has been asking for an apparatus to detect submarines, since the existing apparatus at his disposal has a range of only half a kilometre. He has been told that the Soviet Union has nothing suitable for his requirements.

ii The Airforce. All our airforce pilots . . . know that you possess advanced planes, like the M500, which we had until recently. But with you everything is secret: nobody is allowed to go near them.

iii The Army. Our officers know that you have much more powerful guns than the Americans have, but as usual all this is kept secret, and your experts deny that they exist . . . You treat us as a backward nation which knows nothing about anything. Yet our officers have undergone in your schools exactly the same training as your own officers. We follow all that is going on in the world, East and West.

From Mohammed Heikal, *Sphinx and Commissar: the Rise and Fall of Soviet Influence in the Arab World*, Collins, 1978.

Questions

1 Why do you think the Nile Dam project was so important to a) Egypt and, b) Soviet Russia?

2 What information is there in the sources about Soviet policy towards 'emerging nations' like Egypt?

3 What evidence is there in Source A of President Nasser's dislike of communists?

4 Make a list of President Sadat's criticisms of Soviet policy in his letter.

5 Is there any evidence in Sadat's letter that Soviet Russia had withdrawn only its 'experts'?

6 From Source B, what reasons do you think the USSR might have for being unwilling to supply Egypt with all the arms it wanted?

7 Did Soviet Russia and Egypt trust each other?

8 Look at Source B on page 79. What kind of support was Egypt receiving from Soviet Russia a year after Sadat's letter to Brezhnev?

39 The United States and Israel

US President Truman recognised the independent state of Israel within twenty-four hours of its declaration by the Jewish leader David Ben-Gurion on 14 May 1948. Two years later, the United States signed an agreement called the Tripartite Declaration with Great Britain and France. The three Powers aimed to preserve Israel's boundaries along the cease-fire lines of 1949 and to strengthen the defence of the Middle East against Soviet expansion.

During the Cold War period of the 1950s and 1960s the USA was generally thought to support Israel against revolutionary Arab governments who tended to be backed by the USSR. A Soviet view of American policy appeared in Pravda, *on 27 November 1968. Yet American support for Israel was often cautious, as the autobiography of Moshe Dayan, Israel's defence minister, shows (Source B). He describes Israel's approaches to the United States during the War of Yom Kippur in October 1973.*

A A Soviet view 1968

From *Pravda*, 27 November 1968.

On the piece of paper are the words, 'Arms for Israel'. Underneath the cartoon is written 'Scene at the "Phantom"'

B Israel looks to the United States, October 1973

Our highest priorities were ammunition and aircraft. We kept sending urgent personal cables with detailed and painful explanations of our vital and immediate need for Phantom planes. Only on Tuesday, October 9, three days after the war began, did we get a positive response: we would receive two Phantoms ... The reluctance to give us anything, even a single screw, arose from Washington's information that Israel had started the war and the formidable oil lobby's demand that Israel should not be supported against the Arabs. We were told that only if and when our situation worsened would we be able to get additional arms ...

On Wednesday, the following day, we were informed that the president had approved most of the electronic equipment we had requested, as well as additional planes. He had also decided on a policy of replacement, namely, whatever we lost in battle would be restored. It was explained to us privately that many obstacles had to be overcome before this decision was reached and that our friends hoped that various senators would now cease their criticism.

During that very night and morning, October 9 and 10, more than twenty huge Soviet Antonov transport planes landed on Syrian airfields from Russia. The U.S. government was well aware that the Soviet Union had begun massive airlifts of arms to the Arab states. I thought that America would regard this Russian act with real concern and, in response, would decide to speed up and strengthen their arms supplies to us. And, indeed, starting on October 14, the United States began operating a military airlift ... This was a most impressive supply lift, and it solved the ammunition problem.

From Moshe Dayan, *Story of my Life*, William Morrow and Co. Inc., 1976.

Questions

1 Who do the figures in the cartoon represent?

2 What does the cartoon tell you about a Soviet view of the USA?

3 In which ways do Sources A and B agree about Israel's links with the USA?

4 Why was the United States unwilling at first to help Israel during the war of 1973? What caused her change of mind?

5 What is meant in the first paragraph, Source B, by 'formidable oil lobby'? Why should it be against supplying Israel? How were its fears justified after the 1973 war?

40 The United States and Libya: 1

In 1970 the US abandoned her naval bases in Tripoli, but her relations with the Libyan government remained cool. In 1973, Colonel Qadhafi declared that the Gulf of Sidra (see map, page 83) was Libya's 'internal sea'. Qadhafi's declaration was declared illegal by the United Nations. In 1979, the US embassy in Tripoli was set on fire by a crowd, following the failure of a US operation to rescue American hostages held in Iran. On 6 May 1981, President Reagan ordered Libya to close its embassy in Washington, accusing her of supporting international terrorism. A few months later US aircraft on manoeuvres over the Gulf of Sidra shot down two Soviet-built Libyan SU22 planes which had attacked them.

Between 1983 and 1985, American military forces and civilians in the Mediterranean region were killed in attacks by extremist groups. The US government blamed some of these on Colonel Qadhafi's open support for groups like Abu Nidal's Palestinian Revolutionary Brigade which had attacked airline passengers at Rome and Vienna. In March 1986 more US manoeuvres near the Gulf of Sidra led to the sinking of a Libyan warship, the firing of SAM missiles at US navy planes and the bombing of Libyan missile sites.

In the early hours, Libyan time, of Tuesday 15 April 1986, President Reagan went on US television to explain what had happened a few hours earlier (Source A). During the following days, opinion polls were conducted in Europe and the USA for the US magazine Newsweek, *on the events of 15 April (Source B).*

A Reagan's speech, 14 April 1986

My fellow Americans, at 7 o'clock this evening, Eastern time*, air and naval forces of the United States launched a series of strikes against the headquarters, terrorist facilities and military assets that support Muammar Gadaffi's subversive activities. The attacks were concentrated and carefully targeted to minimize casualties among the Libyan people, with whom we have no quarrel. From initial reports, our forces have succeeded in their mission. Several weeks ago, in New Orleans, I warned Colonel Gadaffi we would hold his regime accountable for any new terrorist attacks launched against American citizens. More recently I made it clear we would respond as soon as we determined conclusively who was responsible for such attacks. On April 5 in West Berlin a terrorist bomb exploded in a night-club frequented by American servicemen. Sergeant Kenneth Ford and a young Turkish woman were killed and 230 others were wounded, among them some 50 American military personnel. This monstrous brutality is but the latest act in Colonel Gadaffi's reign of terror. The evidence is now conclusive that the terrorist bombing of La Belle discotheque was planned and executed under the direct orders of the Libyan regime. On March 25, more than a week before the attack, orders were sent from Tripoli to the Libyan People's Bureau in East Berlin to conduct a terrorist attack against Americans, to cause maximum and indiscriminate casualties. Libya's agents then planted the bomb. On April 4, the People's Bureau

* 2 am Libyan time, 15 April 1986.

From *The Times*, London, 16 April 1986.

alerted Tripoli that the attack would be carried out the following morning. The next day they reported back to Tripoli on the great success of their mission.

Our evidence is direct, it is precise, it is irrefutable. We have solid evidence about other attacks Gadaffi has planned against the United States installations and diplomats and even American tourists . . .

Colonel Gadaffi is not only an enemy of the United States. His record of subversion and aggression against the neighbouring states in Africa is well documented and well known. He has ordered the murder of fellow Libyans in countless countries. He has sanctioned acts of terror in Africa, Europe and the Middle East, as well as the Western hemisphere. Today we have done what we had to do. If necessary, we shall do it again.

B Opinion poll on US action

From *Newsweek*, 28 April 1986.

Do you approve or disapprove of this week's U.S. military action against Libya?

	United States	Great Britain	West Germany	France
Approve	71%	30%	25%	61%
Disapprove	21%	66%	75%	32%
Don't know	8%	4%	0%	7%

In the long run, what effect do you think the U.S. action will have on international terrorism: is terrorist activity likely to increase, decrease or stay about the same?

	United States	Great Britain	West Germany	France
Increase	39%	71%	58%	41%
Decrease	31%	8%	9%	26%
Stay the same	23%	20%	33%	30%
Don't know	7%	1%	0%	3%

Do you think U.S. President Reagan makes wise use of military forces to solve foreign-policy problems or do you think he is too quick to employ U.S. forces?

	United States	Great Britain	West Germany	France
Yes, wise use	62%	18%	21%	47%
No, too quick	26%	77%	76%	47%
Don't know	12%	5%	3%	6%

Which one of the following possible future U.S. actions would you support as the principal means of dealing with Libya?

	United States	Great Britain	West Germany	France
Economic sanctions	34%	57%	44%	41%
Bombing the oilfields	10%	6%	0%	5%
Instigating a military coup	42%	26%	22%	39%
Doing nothing	3%	5%	23%	9%
Don't know	11%	6%	11%	6%

Questions

1 What happened on 14 April?

2 What evidence is there in Source A of Reagan's attitude towards Colonel Qadhafi? Why did Reagan say 'we have no quarrel' with the Libyan people?

3 How might an historian investigate his 'precise' and 'irrefutable' evidence of Libyan involvement?

4 Which of the four polls would most worry President Reagan and his advisers?

5 Explain how the answers to the bottom right-hand poll support the thinking shown in the top left.

6 In what ways does American opinion support US presidential thinking on the raid?

7 How would you explain British, French and German opinions on the US action?

8 Discuss the advantages and disadvantages of opinion polls for understanding events in world affairs.

41 The United States and Libya: 2

President Reagan decided to launch air strikes against Libya on 7 April 1986, after extremists had killed and injured US servicemen in Berlin (see Unit 40). On 11 April, he sent the American ambassador to the United Nations to Western Europe to gain support for the plan. Only the British prime minister, Margaret Thatcher, agreed to help. Reagan finally approved the military operation, code-named El Dorado Canyon, on 13 April. On the evening of 14 April, nearly 60 US fighter bombers and tanker aircraft took off from bases in England. At 2 am local time, Libya's two major cities were attacked from the air. US carrier-based aircraft also took part in the raids. Colonel Qadhafi survived the raid on Tripoli, but one of his children, and, according to a Libyan estimate, more than 100 other Libyans were killed.

Source A is an extract from British journalist Robert Fisk's description of a scene in the Libyan capital the next morning. Source B is from the US weekly magazine, Time.

A After the raid, 15 April 1986

The two-storey homes on both sides of Said bin Zaik Street had been torn apart, their contents of beds, sofas and cheaply framed family photographs hurled into the gardens and draped down sagging bedroom walls.

There was blood across the steps of the bungalow opposite the French embassy, and, on a stretcher down the road, lay part of a baby's body. They had already dug two corpses out of the wreckage of Mohamed Mashirgir's home. Several limbs lay in an ambulance beside a 30 ft. wide waterlogged bomb crater. From a shattered balcony an old man looked down on us, bandages across his cheeks and forehead, blood streaking his shirt. 'Are we terrorists?' he shrieked. 'The Americans are bastards.'

There was real, scarcely controlled fury in the streets of the Bin Ashour suburb of Tripoli yesterday morning, not the remote-controlled anger of Colonel Gadaffi's militia-men, but shouted, cursed insults from ordinary civilians. They had already been told on the radio that Mrs. Thatcher had allowed President Reagan to send some of his bombers from Britain. They knew that Mr. Reagan was claiming to have hit only 'terrorist targets' with pinpoint accuracy. They also realized, of course, he was wrong . . .

A young girl sitting amid the ruins of her sitting room, . . . shaking all the while with the delayed shock of the bomb blast, . . . pointed down the road past the French Embassy, with its smashed windows and shrapnel-gashed facade, to a large gaunt building – perhaps 10 storeys high – almost half a mile away. 'That's the headquarters of the security police,' she said. 'That must have been their target, but they dropped their bombs on us.' The Japanese Ambassador, Mr. Eija Tanaka, standing outside his own windowless embassy, said the same thing.

From *The Times*, London, 16 April 1986.

The group of Gadaffi officials who took the press to this scene of devastation did not, of course, allude to the grim and scarcely damaged building across the rubble. Nor did the young gunman who emerged want television crews to film in that direction. The killing of civilians, they said, was a wanton act of Anglo–American aggression – and 'Anglo–American aggression' is the expression they are using now.

B

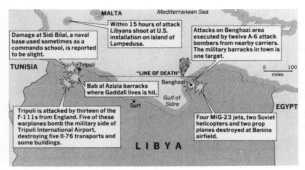

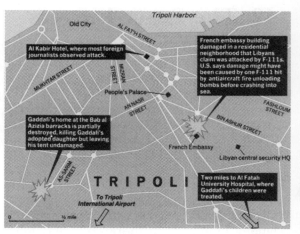

Major targets in Libya (above)
Close-up on Tripoli (right)

From *Time*, 28 April 1986.

Questions

1 What do Sources A and B tell you about US reasons for the raid?

2 List details of the raid mentioned in Fisk's report but left out of the maps. Suggest some reasons for these omissions.

3 How far do these sources support or disprove the first two sentences in Source A, Unit 40?

4 Can you identify from the sources the target the US warplanes missed? Why did a gunman not want television crews filming 'in that direction'?

5 Why were Libyans using the phrase 'Anglo–American aggression'?

6 After the raid, the Soviet Union accused the United States of an 'act of aggression'. How would the US government have defended its attack?

7 How far are A and B reliable historical sources?

8 What conclusions might an historian reach on the effects of the raid, using the sources above and the opinion poll on Page 81?

Part 8

Tensions

42 The Peace-keepers

After the Suez War of 1956 Egypt agreed to a United Nations Emergency Force (UNEF) keeping the peace in Sinai and Gaza (Source C). On 18 May 1967 the Egyptians asked the UNEF to leave. Source A is a journalist's eye-witness account of a departure ceremony in Gaza. A few weeks later, war broke out between Israel and her neighbours. In Source B, the United Nations Secretary General, U Thant, reports to the Security Council about attacks on the few UNEF troops who had not been withdrawn on the first day of the war.

A Withdrawal, 1967

On the border of the Gaza Strip today I watched the sad little ceremony of UNO's withdrawal – and tonight, for the first time in 10 years, the symbol of the blue-helmeted peace troops between Egyptians and Israelis is missing. This was the scene from Erez on the Israel side. Behind me stood a tight little group of Israeli soldiers . . . Fifty yards in front the UNO troops – Canadians, Swedes, Yugoslavs, Indians, Danes – hauled down their flag as a Sikh band in red ceremonial uniforms played a rousing English march. Beyond them, in the orange groves, Egyptian soldiers were already taking position in trenches. I could also see a swarm of Arabs being held back by Egyptian troops. There was no sign of the 'huge' force of armour and guns the Israelis say has been lurking in the Sinai Desert. Jeeps of the UNO force kept coming into this checkpoint from isolated observation posts along the rest of the 170 mile border and coastal strip between Egypt and Israel.

From *Daily Express*, London, 20 May 1967.

B 5 June 1967

The Commander of UNEF (Rikye) reported that at 12.45 hours local time . . . Israeli artillery opened fire on two camps of the Indian contingent of UNEF, which were . . . being abandoned, and soon thereafter the United Arab Republic tanks surrounded one of the camps which still contains one reduced Indian company.

General Rikye also reported that a UNEF convoy . . . on the road between Gaza and Rafah was strafed by an Israeli aircraft . . . although . . . all UNEF vehicles are painted white . . . Three Indian soldiers were killed and an unknown number were wounded . . .

From U Thant, *View from the UN*, David Charles, 1978.

C

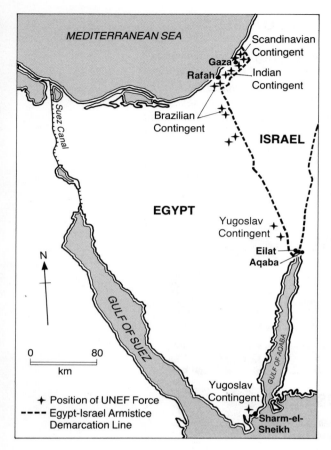

UNEF in Egypt, May 1967

Map legend:
- MEDITERRANEAN SEA
- Gaza
- Rafah
- Scandinavian Contingent
- Indian Contingent
- Brazilian Contingent
- ISRAEL
- EGYPT
- Suez Canal
- Yugoslav Contingent
- Eilat
- Aqaba
- N
- GULF OF SUEZ
- GULF OF AQABA
- Yugoslav Contingent
- Sharm-el-Sheikh
- 0 ─ 80 km
- ✛ Position of UNEF Force
- ----- Egypt-Israel Armistice Demarcation Line

Questions

1 Using information from all the sources, make a list of a) ways in which UNEF soldiers, vehicles and positions could be identified, and b) the nations who had sent troops to join UNEF.

2 Why is the line separating Egypt and Israel described as a 'border' in Source A, but as an 'Armistice Demarcation Line' on the map?

3 Can you think of reasons why Israel refused to allow UNEF forces on its side of the line?

4 Why does the *Daily Express* journalist in Source B refer to the withdrawal ceremony as 'sad'?

5 Do the sources suggest any reasons for the attack on UN forces on 5 June?

6 Think of yourself as a UN soldier helping to keep the peace. Using information from the sources, write a letter home telling of your work and experiences in Egypt.

43 Freedom fighters or terrorists?

On 5 September 1972, an armed PLO group, calling itself 'Black September', attacked the Israeli team at the Munich Olympics. They killed two Israeli athletes and held nine others during a siege seen worldwide on television and in the evening papers (Source A). Sources B and C are from Black September's demands and the Israeli ambassador's reply. Late in the evening the West German police fought a gun battle with the Palestinians while an aircraft waited to fly them and the hostages to the Middle East. Five out of eight Palestinians and all the hostages were killed. Black September's operation was justified in the memoirs (Source D) of Abu Jihad, a PLO official killed by Israeli agents in Tunis in 1988. Yasser Arafat gave his views on terrorism in his 1974 speech to the UN (Source E).

A

 London Tuesday September 5, 1972 No. 28,177 3p **Evening News**

Arabs shoot two Israelis dead, seize athletes

ASSASSINATION AT THE OLYMPICS

THE MAN WHO GOT AWAY — Weightlifting coach Tuvia Sokolovsky. He escaped through a window.

Then hour-by-hour drama of hostages

From IAIN MACDONALD and News Agencies
MUNICH, Tuesday.

ARAB terrorists armed with machine-guns broke into the Olympic village early today, killed two Israeli team members and held 26 other Israeli athletes and officials hostage.

Then, according to reports broadcast from Israel, they threatened to shoot one Israeli every two hours if Israel did not agree to free more than 200 guerilla prisoners.

The Arabs set a noon deadline. Tension mounted. But noon came and went . . . and then the ultimatum was extended, first to 1 p.m. and then to 5 p.m.

As negotiations went on, and a "hot line" was opened between Munich and Jerusalem, one of the dead men was named as 28-year-old Moshe Weinberg, the Israeli squad's wrestling trainer and a former leading wrestling champion. He was married and the father of a two-month-old boy.

Four of the hostages were named as Andre Spitzer, fencing trainer; Kehat Shorr, shooting; Yosef Gottfreund, wrestling; and Amitzur Shapira, athletics.

An Israeli journalist said Weinberg was shot in bed after the Arabs, who climbed a fence, broke into the Olympic Village. Their faces were blacked and one of them was said to be a woman. Sources put the number of terrorists at between five and nine.

EX-CHAMPION WHO DIED . . AND THE MEN WHO FACE 'WE WILL KILL ONE EVERY TWO HOURS' THREAT

MOSHE WEINBERG, an Israeli wrestling coach, who was killed by the gunmen.

 ANDRE SPITZER Fencing Coach

AMITZUR SHAPIRA Athletics Coach

  KEHAT SHORR Marksmanship Coach

EVENING NEWS MEN ON THE SPOT
How police

THE WEATHER

The Meteorological Office forecasts:

UNTIL NOON TOMORROW: Dry, rather cloudy at times, sunny spells; wind north to north-east, moderate, falling light at times; temperatures near normal, maximum 20 degrees C. (68 degrees F.)

INLAND, SOUTH-EAST ENGLAND, EAST ANGLIA, CENTRAL SOUTHERN ENGLAND, E. MIDLANDS, CHANNEL ISLANDS, SOUTH-WEST ENGLAND, MIDLANDS, WALES, NORTH SEA, STRAITS OF DOVER.

B Black September's demands, 5 September 1972

1 The German Federal Republic must announce that it agrees to have the Israeli prisoners transferred to any other location designated by our revolutionary forces in Olympic Village.

2 The G.F.R. must put at the disposal of our forces three airplanes on which the Israeli prisoners and our armed forces will fly . . .

3 Any attempt to sabotage our operation will result in immediate liquidation of all the Israeli prisoners, for which the G.F.R. will bear total responsibility . . .

From Serge Groussard, *The Blood of Israel*, William Morrow and Company Inc., 1973.

C Israel's reply

If we once give way to blackmail, hijackings and kidnappings will multiply infernally . . . Every one of us has been explicitly warned: in no case can we serve as bargaining counters. After all, we are at war. Every kidnapping, every commando attack is regarded as a military engagement in which we Israelis, soldiers or civilians, risk losing our lives. We do not bargain, but we must defend ourselves. That means, in this case, that there must be an immediate counter-attack.

From David Hirst, *The Gun and the Olive Branch*, Faber and Faber, 1983.

D The PLO explains

At the beginning of 1972 the PLO in an official letter to the Olympic Committee asked for a Palestinian team to be allowed to compete in the Olympic Games. There was no reply, so a second letter was sent . . . – the only response was contemptuous silence. This worthy organization, which claims to be non-political, obviously considered us to be non-existent . . .

'Black September' decided to take this matter into their own hands and devised a plan with three aims: first, to underline the existence of the Palestinian people: second, to use the many international press representatives in Munich to gain a hearing – positive or negative, it did not matter – for our cause throughout the world; third, to force Israel to release 200 resistance fighters.

From Abdallah Frangi, *The P.L.O. and Palestine*, Zed Books Ltd., 1983.

E Arafat on terrorism

The difference between the revolutionary and the terrorist lies in the reason for which each fights. For whoever stands by a just cause and fights for the freedom and liberation of his land from the invaders, the settlers, and the colonialists, cannot possibly be called terrorist . . . those who fight against the just causes, those who wage war to occupy, colonize and oppress other people – those are the terrorists . . .

From W. Laqueur and B. Rubin (eds.), *The Israel–Arab Reader* (4th Edition), Facts on File Publications, 1985.

Questions

1 Why did Black September claim that the Germans would be responsible for the Israelis' deaths?

2 Why would the Israelis not bargain?

3 From Source D what seems to be the most important excuse for the attack?

4 Was the second aim in D achieved in reports such as that in the *Evening News*?

5 What evidence in B and D might be used to support Arafat's definition of a 'revolutionary'?

6 How would an Israeli argue, using the sources, that Black September's aims and methods could not be called 'just'?

44 Oil Crisis

Oil was discovered in large quantities in 1908 in southern Persia. After the First World War rich fields were found in Iraq, Kuwait, Bahrain and Saudi Arabia. British, French and American oil companies gained control of production on cheap terms. By the 1950s nearly all the oil states were independent and took a 50 per cent share of profits. Yet the price fell because the companies cut their costs to compensate for taxes on petrol and because the Arab countries allowed large quantities to be drilled. Arab discontent with falling oil prices was heightened by dislike of the support from the western states for Israel. This came to a head during the October War in 1973. Sources A and B are reports of decisions made by OAPEC – the Organisation for Arab Petroleum Exporting Countries. Source C quotes Sheik Yamani, the oil minister of Saudi Arabia, when his biographer asked about the use of oil as a weapon. The table shows what four countries earned from oil, 1972–86.

A OAPEC statement, 17 October 1973

For the third time there is a war resulting from Israel's defiance of our legitimate rights with the backing and support of the United States. This prompts the Arabs to adopt a decision not to continue to make economic sacrifices by producing quantities of their vital oil wealth in excess of what is justified by the economic factors in their states unless the world community moves to put matters in order, compel Israel to withdraw from our occupied lands, and make the United States aware of the exorbitant price the great industrial states are paying as a result of its blind and unbounded support for Israel.

Therefore, the Arab Oil Ministers meeting on 17 October in the city of Kuwait have decided immediately to begin reducing production in every Arab oil-producing country by no less than five per cent of the production for the month of September. The same procedure will be applied every month and production will be reduced by the same percentage of the previous month's production until the Israeli forces are completely evacuated from all the Arab territories occupied in the June 1967 war and the legitimate rights of the Palestine people are restored.

From T. G. Fraser, *The Middle East, 1914–1979*, Edward Arnold, 1980.

B OAPEC meeting, 5 November 1973

The total reduction of production by every Arab state which implemented the decision shall be 25% of the production of the month of September, including the quantities deducted as a result of cutting off supplies to the United States and the Dutch market . . .

From T. G. Fraser (ed.), *The Middle East, 1914–1979*, Edward Arnold, 1980.

C 'The oil weapon'

Why do you refer to it as the oil weapon? Why don't you think of it the way we did, as a political instrument? A weapon is used to hurt people. A political instrument is used to make a political point and hopefully affect political change. We did not believe in the use of oil as a weapon because we knew this was not the best way for true cooperation with the west, notably the United States. But King Faisal* saw American policies in the Middle East as being so very one-sided. He said to the west on several occasions that he wanted the United States to negotiate on Israel's behalf to find a solution to the Palestinian situation and the Israeli occupation of Arab territories seized in the June War six years previous. Oil as a political weapon was saved as a last resort measure only to make that happen.

From Jeffrey Robinson, *Yamani: the inside story*, S. Schuster, 1988.

* of Saudi Arabia

D Incomes in millions of US dollars, 1972–86

	1972	1974	1976	1978	1980	1982	1984	1986
Iran	$2308	22000	22000	20900	11600	19000	15000	5000
Saudi Arabia	$3107	29000	33500	36700	104200	76000	43700	20000
Iraq	$ 575	6000	8500	11600	26500	9500	10400	7000
Libya	$1598	6000	7500	9300	23200	14000	10400	5000

From *Middle East and North Africa, 1983* and *1987*, Europa Press Publications, 1983, 1987.

Questions

1 Which oil-producing Middle East state appears to be the most powerful?

2 From Source A, explain a) why the OAPEC states cut oil production and, b) what they meant by 'economic sacrifices'.

3 What did OAPEC decide to do on 17 October? What further action had been taken by November?

4 Write a letter to a newspaper, putting a different view on the 'oil weapon' from Sheik Yamani's.

5 Suggest some difficulties that OAPEC might have had in putting the decisions into effect.

6 How does Source D suggest that oil revenues were affected by the decisions in 1973? Can you think of another OAPEC action that affected the trend in oil revenues?

7 What does Source D tell you about the possible effects of a) the Iranian revolution, b) the Gulf War and c) a world economic recession?

45 Lebanon collapses

In 1976 Lebanon's population was estimated at 2 million. About 43 per cent were Christian Arabs (chiefly Maronite Catholics), about 44 per cent were Arab Muslims (in two main groups, the Shias and Sunnis) and about 7 per cent were Druzes, an ancient offshoot of the Muslim faith. When Lebanon became independent in 1944 the communities agreed a form of power sharing. The compromise remained in force until the early 1970s when some Muslim groups and left-wing Arab nationalists such as the Druzes' Social Progressive Society (PPS) led by Kamal Joumblatt, and the Nasserites, began to try to limit Christian power. By that time there were about 400,000 Palestinian refugees in Lebanon. Their camps sheltered the heavily armed Fatah (or Fath). Their raids into Israel led to Israeli reprisals into Lebanon. Inside Lebanon the Palestinians gave their support to the Muslim and nationalist groups who, in turn, backed the PLO claim for united Arab action against Israel. Lebanese Christian groups were moving towards closer support for Israel. In April 1975 civil war broke out after right-wing Christians massacred twenty-six Palestinians in a Beirut bus.

The map shows how Lebanon was divided. Source B is from a journal kept by the American wife of a Lebanese businessman who describes life in West Beirut during the civil war. She uses capital letters instead of names of friends. Later in April 1976, the Syrians sent troops into Lebanon to end the war.

A Lebanon divided, 1976

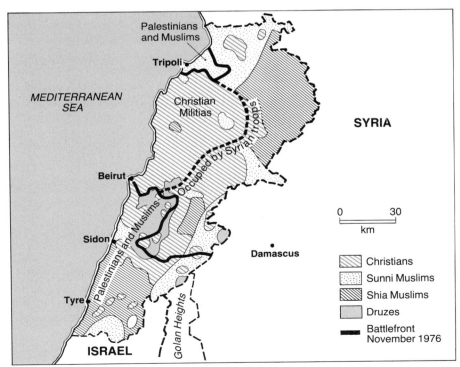

B Life in Beirut, March–April 1976

March 21: 1.00 pm. The battle begins in the hotel district – sounds of distant firing, machine gun, rifle shots ring out, soon to be beneath the thunder of cannons and rockets. We are engulfed in storm and thunder, but the boys sleep . . .

From David C. Gordon, *Lebanon: The Fragmented Nation*, Croom Helm Ltd., 1980.

March 22: . . . 4.00 am. A loudspeaker truck tours the empty street asking for blood donations. But who dares venture out of his house to give? . . .

April 1: Monday, Tuesday, Wednesday pass in uneventful waiting and endless political discussion:

B: 'My sources tell me that there will be a new president in 24 hours.'

C: 'The conflict has been internationalized . . .'

B: 'It's all a plot between Joumblatt and the Maronites to destroy the Palestinian resistance.'

C: 'No! It's a plot by the Americans to solve the Middle East question at the expense of Lebanon.'

D: 'Joumblatt is crazy.'

E: 'It's all a Lebanese political power struggle to see who will be the next president . . .'

That same evening the family F had some 'visitors'. A delegation of PPS gunmen came asking for G. Soon a 'delegation' from Fath and one from the Nasserites, accompanied by a cannon mounted on the back of a truck, joined them . . . they all, about 25, carefully searched the house and then politely left. As they did so, Mrs. H, as a proper hostess, offered them candy.

April 2: I called from Ashrafiyya (E Beirut). She has no electricity. Fresh fruits and vegetables, so abundant here (West Beirut) do not exist in Ashrafiyya. Yesterday 'They' demanded 30,000 L.L.* from her brother-in-law.

* Lebanese pounds

April 3: Afternoon: . . . A stops to introduce C to the Fath guards and to thank them for retrieving the ball which is constantly landing on them from the balcony . . . They point to the labour of the day, newly painted Arabic letters saying 'Fath' and 'Fath Arab Revolution' decorating the stone frame above the K building doorway. Thus is Fath protection of this building guaranteed . . .

Questions

1 From A, suggest why it was difficult to end the civil war.

2 In Source B what evidence is there that West Beirut was cut off from the outside world?

3 How does B suggest that law and order had broken down?

4 What does the political discussion suggest about people's difficulty in understanding the war? Can you explain the meaning of C's remarks?

5 As a foreign journalist in Beirut in 1976, write a short report explaining what it was like there and how difficult it was to get accurate information.

46 Revolution in Iran

The Shah of Iran and his family went into exile on 16 January 1979 when he could no longer resist opposition to his rule. His programme of industrial and agricultural modernisation, introduced in 1961 and paid for by Iran's expanding oil industry, had failed to satisfy his critics who thought the Shah's rule was un-Islamic, corrupt and pro-Western. Most Iranian Muslims are Shias who believe that the leaders of the Islamic faith are the religious descendants of Ali, the son-in-law of the Prophet Mohammed. They believe that an Ayatollah, meaning 'sign of God' is the only correct interpreter of the Koran. A powerful opponent of the Shah was an Ayatollah, Mousavi Khomeini, who was forced into exile in France in December 1963. From France he became an important leader of opposition to the Shah. He returned two weeks after the Shah's flight, when civil war had broken out between the revolutionaries and supporters of the Shah. By mid-February 1979, the revolutionaries had gained the upper hand and formed a new government under Shia control. Source A is from an eye-witness account by a French journalist, Dominique Pouchin, who worked in Isfahan, Iran's second largest city, in February 1979.

Ayatollah Khomeini was named in the 1979 constitution of the Islamic Republic of Iran as its religious leader. In Source B, he is shown on 3 November 1980, addressing young Shia militia-men who had been holding 53 United States embassy staff hostage in Tehran since 4 November 1979. Khomeini died on 3 June 1989.

A The Islamic revolution

The city is calm, though the revolution has well and truly arrived. It was only the noon prayer meeting on Friday which disturbed the tranquility. Some 90,000 men sat crosslegged on their prayer mats laid out on the huge mosque area fenced in by an ochre wall. They sat in hundreds of straight rows facing a gigantic picture of Ayatollah Khomeini, which was reversed by some 60 men when the praying started, for 'you pray only to God'. The women, all veiled, stood on the other side of an endless white sheet which served as a wall. Loud-speakers fixed at intervals of 100 metres on posts gave out the 'good word'.

Ayatollah Taheri* harangued the people who replied at regular intervals raising their fists: 'You are right, Khomeini is our leader.' 'Will you let the foreigner command our country and our army?' he asked. 'No,' shouted the crowd, 'we want the Islamic revolution and Allah's party.'

As night fell, Isfahan's streets emptied. The last of the homeward-bound citizens were stopped and checked by the Islamic police patrols. In the narrow covered alleyways of the Old Bazaar, young men armed with clubs and iron bars strutted about. All carried cards bearing Ayatollah Khademi's* signature pinned to their jacket lapels. In a neighbouring mosque, a score of other young men waited for their duty turn. The duty roster hung on the wall. Everything was going smoothly at the 'police station'. Isfahan was deep in slumber.

From The Guardian Weekly, *18 February 1979.*

* *local Shia Muslim leaders*

B Ayatollah Khomeini addresses a meeting

The sign on the wall behind Khomeini is the Farsi word 'Allah'. Standing next to Khomeini is his son, Ahmad

Questions

1 What does the journalist mean when she says that 'the revolution has well and truly arrived' in Isfahan?

2 In Source A, why does Taheri appear to be biased against 'the foreigner'?

3 Are there any signs in Source A that not everyone was happy with the revolution?

4 Do you think that Ayatollah Khomeini's position in the hall had been thought out beforehand?

5 Suggest some reasons for the presence of Khomeini's surviving son.

6 How does Source B add to the journalist's description of the ways in which Khomeini and his followers wished to be seen, heard and obeyed?

7 Which of Sources A or B provides the historian with more reliable evidence of Khomeini's importance to the Iranian revolution?

47 The Iraq–Iran War

The Iran–Iraq frontier was disputed for centuries until 6 March 1975 when the two countries signed a treaty. It made changes in the frontier, including moving it from the Iranian side of the Shatt-al-Arab waterway to mid-channel. The two also agreed not to interfere in each other's internal affairs. Before, they had accused each other of helping rebels among the Kurdish people who lived on each side of the northern boundaries.

After the Iranian Revolution in February 1979, tension grew and there were border clashes in summer 1980. On 17 September President Hussein of Iraq cancelled the 1975 agreement (Source A). Five days later Iraq's armed forces invaded Iran. On 30 September Ayatollah Khomeini spoke on Iranian radio (Source B) in reply to Iraq's offer of a cease-fire.

In 1982, Iranian forces counter-attacked into Iraq. Iraq extended the war into the Gulf by attacking ships which entered a maritime exclusion zone. Both sides then fought bloody military campaigns and attacked towns, oil installations and Gulf shipping with bombs and missiles. Source C is a photograph of a wall-mural showing President Hussein that appeared in Tehran in 1986. In 1987, foreign countries sent warships to the Gulf to protect their merchant vessels. In April 1988 Iraq launched a fresh land offensive and on 18 July President Khamenei sent a letter to the UN Secretary General (Source D), accepting a Security Council resolution for a cease-fire made a year earlier. Iraq had accepted it at the outset.

A Hussein challenges Iran, 17 September 1980

Since the rulers of Iran have violated this agreement as of the beginning of their reign by blatantly and deliberately intervening in Iraq's domestic affairs by backing and financing, as did the Shah before them, the leaders of the mutiny* . . . which is backed by America and Zionism, and by refusing to return the Iraqi territories, which we were compelled to liberate by force, I announce before you that we consider the 6 March 1975 agreement as abrogated* . . . the legal relationship concerning Shatt-al-Arab should return to what it was before 6 March 1975. This Shatt shall again be, as it has been throughout history, Iraqi and Arab in name and reality, with all rights of full sovereignty over it.

From R. K. Ramazani, *Revolutionary Iran: challenge and response in the Middle East*, John Hopkins University Press, 1987.
* *Kurdish rebellion*

* *cancelled*

B Ayatollah Khomeini replies

Saddam Hussein has extended his hand to compromise with us. We will not compromise with him. He is an infidel, a person who is corrupt, a perpetrator of corruption. We will fight against them right to the end, and, God willing, shall be victorious. We shall pay no attention to any of the governments who might assist him . . . Our duty is to safeguard and protect Islam . . . Even if we are killed it will not matter, and if we kill, God willing, we shall attain paradise.

From *New York Times*, 1 October 1980.

C An Iranian viewpoint

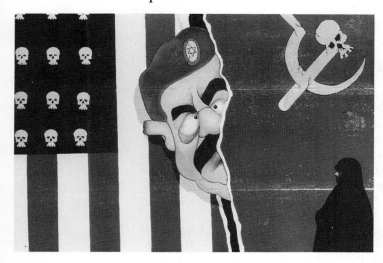

A woman wearing a chador, *or veil,*
stands in front of the mural

D Iran accepts the cease-fire

. . . the fire of the war which was started by the Iraqi regime on 22
September 1980 through an aggression against the territorial integrity
of the Islamic Republic of Iran has now gained unprecedented dimen-
sions, bringing other countries into the war and even engulfing
innocent civilians . . . The killing of 290 innocent human beings,
caused by the shooting down of an Airbus aircraft of the Islamic
Republic of Iran by one of the American warships in the Persian Gulf,
is a clear manifestation of this contention . . .

   . . . the Islamic Republic of Iran – because of the importance it
attaches to saving the lives of human beings and the establishment of
justice and regional and international peace and security – accepts
Security Council Resolution 598 . . .'

From *The Times*,
London, 19 July 1988.

Questions

1 What do A and B reveal
about the causes of the war?

2 Is there a clue in A to why
most Arab countries backed
Iraq?

3 To which countries do the
flags and the emblem in
Hussein's cap in C refer?

4 What effect might the mural
have as anti-Iraqi propaganda?

5 Why does D refer to the
shooting down of an airliner?

6 Can you think why Iraq and
Iran should accuse each
other of receiving help from
the same countries?

7 What evidence is there in
Sources B, C and D that
Iran believed she was
fighting a 'religious' war?

8 Does Source D modify in any
way what Ayatollah
Khomeini said in Source B?

Acknowledgements

We are grateful to the following for permission to reproduce copyright material:

Express Newspapers plc for an extract from the article 'Blue Helmets exit, to music' by Robin Stafford in *Daily Express* 20.5.67; Guardian News Services Ltd for an extract from the article 'Panic at the Wailing Wall' in *The Guardian* 12.10.87; Molly Lyons Bar-David for an extract from *My Promised Land*; Princeton University Press for extracts from pp 801–2 from *The Old Social Classes and the Revolutionary Movements of Iraq* 1st edition 1978. by H. Batatu; Times Newspapers Ltd for an extract from the article 'Myth of surgical bombing' by Robert Fisk in *The Times* 16.4.86. © Times Newspapers Ltd 1986; The Women's Press for an extract from *Memoirs from the Women's Prison* by Nawal el Sa'adawi.

We are grateful to the following for permission to reproduce photographs: Ancient Art & Architecture Collection, page 10; Barnabys Picture Library, page 55; BIPAC, pages 21, 38; British Library, pages 6, 13; *Evening News*, 5.9.1972, page 86 (photo: John Frost); *The Guardian*, 20.9.1982, page 67 (L. Gibbard); Hulton Deutsche Collection, page 15; The Illustrated London News Picture Library, pages 25, 39; Library of Congress, page 74; London Express News & Feature Service, page 37; Popperfoto, pages 45, 93; Frank Spooner, page 95 (photo: Pascal Maitre); Topham Picture Library, page 57; U.N. Photo, page 41; UNRWA, page 70 (photo: Myrtle Winter Chaumeny).

We are unable to trace the copyright holders of the following and would be grateful for any information that would enable us to do so, pages 9, 31, 33 & 78 (photos by permission of the Syndics of Cambridge University Library), pages 34, 60 & 63 (photos School of Oriental & African Studies).

Cover: A Palestinian refugee camp showing a mother taking her baby to the UNRWA Infant Health Clinic for its weekly check-up. UNRWA (photo: George Nemeh).